920

Honky

University of California Press   *Berkeley   Los Angeles   London*

Honky

Dalton Conley

University of California Press
Berkeley and Los Angeles, California

University of California Press, Ltd.
London, England

Library of Congress Cataloging-in-Publication Data

Conley, Dalton, 1969–
    Honky / Dalton Conley.
        p. cm.
    ISBN 0-520-21586-9 (cloth : alk. paper)
    1. White children—New York (State)—New
York—Social conditions. 2. Whites—New York
(State)—New York—Race identity. 3. Whites—
New York (State)—New York—Biography. 4. Afro-
American children—New York (State)—New
York—Social conditions. 5. Hispanic American chil-
dren—New York (State)—New York—Social condi-
tions. 6. Race awareness in children—New York
(State)—New York. 7. Social classes—New York
(State)—New York—History—20th century.
8. Lower East Side (New York, N.Y.)—Social
conditions. I. Title.

HQ792.U5 C66 2000
305.26'09747—dc21   00-023774
CIP

Manufactured in the United States of America

9   8   7   6   5   4   3   2   1
10   9   8   7   6   5   4   3   2

The paper used in this publication meets the
minimum requirements of ANSI / NISO Z39
0.48-1992(R 1997) (Permanence of Paper). ∞

For Jerome

"Your mother is so white,
she went to her own wedding naked."

Contents

I am not your typical middle-class white male. I am middle class, despite the fact that my parents had no money; I am white, but I grew up in an inner-city housing project where most everyone was black or Hispanic. I enjoyed a range of privileges that were denied my neighbors but that most Americans take for granted. In fact, my childhood was like a social science experiment: Find out what being middle class really means by raising a kid from a so-called good family in a so-called bad neighborhood. Define whiteness by putting a light-skinned kid in the midst of a community of color. If the exception proves the rule, I'm that exception.

Ask any African American to list the adjectives that describe them and they will likely put *black* or *African American* at the top of the list. Ask someone of European descent the same question and *white* will be far down the list, if it's there at all. Not so for me. I've studied whiteness the way I would a foreign language. I know its grammar, its parts of speech; I know the subtleties of its idioms, its vernacular words and phrases to which the native speaker has never given a second thought. There's an old saying that you never really know your own language until you study another. It's the same with race and class.

In fact, race and class are nothing more than a set of stories we tell ourselves to get through the world, to organize our reality. And there was no one who told more stories to me than my mother, Ellen. One of her favorites was how I had wanted a baby sister so badly that I kidnapped a black child in the playground of the housing complex. She told this story each time my real sister, Alexandra, and I were standing, arms crossed, facing away from each other after some squabble or fistfight. The moral of the story for my mother was that I should love my sister, since I had wanted to have her so desperately. The message I took away, however, was one of race. I was fascinated that I could have been oblivious to something that years later feels so natural, so innate as race does . . .

As my mother tells it, the week before I kidnapped the black baby I broke free from her in the supermarket, ran to the back of the last aisle, and grabbed the manager's microphone. "I want a baby sister," I announced, my almost-three-year-old voice reverberating off ceiling-high stacks of canned Goya beans.

"I want a baby sister," I repeated, evidently intrigued by the fact that my own voice seemed to be coming from everywhere. Soon my mother's shopping cart was rattling across the floor of the refrigerated back row where all the meats were kept. I can envision the two long braids on either side of her head flapping maniacally, as if they were wings trying to lift her and the cart off the ground. She was, in fact, pregnant. She had explained to me what this meant a week earlier, and I had become fixated on it, asking each day how much longer it would be. My parents tolerated this first of my many obsessions, happy that at least I was not resentful and jealous, though they wondered why I so much wanted the baby to be a girl and not another something like myself.

"How old will I be when the baby's born?" I asked one day. The next morning I continued my questioning: "When I'm five, how old will the baby be?" Soon after that I started to worry about its sex: "When will we know it's a sister and not a brother?" Skin color never entered my line of questioning.

My parents did their best to engage my curiosity, each in their own way. While my father, Steve, used colored pens to handicap the *Racing Form*, he gave me some markers and told me to draw a picture of the baby. I rushed through this endeavor using only the black marker and produced something that looked like his sweat-smeared copy of the *Form* after a long day at the racetrack. Steve, a painter, had just gotten into a black-and-white phase himself and was touched by my colorless effort; he pinned it up on the wall above the dining room table, where it hung for years.

In contrast to my father, with his visual orientation, my mother, a writer, took a verbal approach. She instructed me to think of an adjective for each letter of the alphabet to describe how I would like my younger sibling to be. We only got through "a-door-bell," my word for *adorable*, and then to *brown* before I got exasperated and insisted that she tell me what the baby would be like—as if she knew and was holding out on me.

Finally, I could stand the wait no longer. About a week after the supermarket incident, I swiped a baby myself. While playing in our housing project's courtyard, I found an unattended stroller. In it was a toddler just a few months younger than me, with cornrows braided so tightly on her little head that they pulled the skin on her face tautly upward. I remember that she was smiling up at me, and I must have taken this as permission. I reached up to grab the handles of the carriage, pushed it across the shards of broken green and brown malt liquor bottles that littered the concrete, and proudly delivered it to my mother, who was sitting on a bench with a neighbor.

"I found my baby sister," I declared, jamming the stroller into her shin for emphasis.

"No you haven't," my mother replied, putting her hand over her open mouth. She turned to her neighbor on the splintered green bench. "Do you know where her mother is?"

The child's parents—leaders of the neighborhood black separatist organization—lived in our building, on our very floor. By now the baby was crying, and I was jumping up and down with excitement, laughing with delight at my success. But my laughter soon dissolved into tears, for my mother immediately seized the plastic handles of the stroller and returned it from where it came. She made a beeline across the concrete, over the black rubber tiles of the kiddie area and under the jungle gym, all the way to the other side of the playground, where a woman was pacing frantically back and forth, her Muslim head scarf flowing out behind her like a proud national flag. When my mother finally reached the woman she apologized repeatedly, explaining that she could certainly empathize with the experience, since I escaped from her sight several times a week. The woman said nothing, her silent glare through narrowed eyes a powerful statement in itself, while the baby and I went on screaming and crying a cacophonous chorus.

After the kidnapping, the separatist mother did not speak to us for a month, as if we had confirmed her worst suspicions about white people. Then, just as the springtime buds were starting to blossom, she talked to my mother in the elevator. "April is the cruelest month," she said, as if T. S. Eliot were code for something. Whenever my mother would tell this part of the story, her voice would soften and trail off. Only later did I figure out that she remembered it so vividly out of a sense of liberal, racial guilt—guilt over her surprise at hearing a black separatist recite English poetry.

"Yes, it is," my mother responded, wracking her brain as she tried to remember which poet had said that. She thought maybe it was Ezra Pound, the Nazi sympathizer, and that the woman was making a veiled expression of anti-Semitism. Then she quoted the poem back to the woman: "Winter kept us warm, covering Earth in forgetful snow . . ."

The woman didn't say anything else, continuing to stare at the numbers as they descended from twenty-one; she got off the elevator at the ground floor and smiled at my mother. At this point in the telling, my mother's voice would rise with the satisfaction that she and the woman had shared a moment, a literary bond. But later that night, well after midnight, the woman, her husband, and my ersatz baby sister were dragging, wheeling, and pushing all of their belongings across the hall-way to the elevator in a caravan of suitcases, each one over-stuffed and bulging, as pregnant with mystery as my mother was with my imminent sibling. The woman was screaming at her husband to hurry up, so loudly that she woke up several families. Parents poked their heads out of steel doorways, blinking as they peered into the fluorescent hallway. Finally my mother asked the woman to keep it down, since we were trying to sleep. I imagine that she asked sheepishly, cowed by her chronic white guilt.

"Noise?" the woman yelled back as she pushed a shopping cart full of overstuffed manila folders down the corridor. Her eyes were as wide with adrenaline as they had been narrowed with seething rage the month before. "The noise is your kid's Big Wheel going up and down, up and down the hallway all day. Don't tell *me* about noise." Despite her reaction, the din soon ebbed, and all that was left of the separatists was a quite literal paper trail that led back to their apartment, whose glossy, brown-painted door stood ajar. I don't need my mother's storytelling to recall the open door. An open door in that neighborhood was something strange and unusual. It usually meant something was seriously amiss—that a woman was fleeing an abusive husband, that a robbery or even a murder had taken place. For me, the open door came to have the same association with death that a hat on a bed does for many people.

Insomniac that she was, my mother stayed up and waited eagerly for the sound of the newspaper dropping outside our door. She savored her morning ritual, in which she brewed dark-roast Bustello-brand Puerto Rican coffee to accompany the *Daily News*. That morning my mother read in the paper that the separatist group had taken credit for a bomb planted at the Statue of Liberty the day before. The bomb had been defused, but it still caused a panic among the tourists. Just as she was reading that the FBI was searching for the members of the separatist group, the racket in the hallway started up again. She peeked out, and there, as if arriving on cue, were the investigators from the FBI, identified by the large yellow letters on the backs of their nylon jackets. Within an hour they, too, had cleared out, padlocking the family's door and pasting layer upon layer of tape over it, yellow strips with black writing that formed negatives of the jackets they had worn. The tape read CRIME SCENE, DO NOT ENTER—as if we had a choice. I was fascinated with this tape and peeled it off strip by strip when I played in the hallway. My mother saved some for my room, guessing correctly that I would like it after a few years, when I understood what it meant. A couple of months later the padlock and tape came down, and a few weeks after that a Chinese family moved in. We never saw the FBI again, and the FBI never saw the separatists.

In retrospect, my baby-seizing mistake was understandable. The idea that a brown-skinned baby couldn't come from two ashen parents wouldn't have entered the mind of a two-and-a-half-year-old. After all, a young child has not yet learned the determinants of skin color, much less the fact that in America families are for the most part organized by skin color. Moreover, in the projects people seemed to come in all colors, shapes, and sizes, and I was not yet aware which were the important ones that divided up the world. At that age, the fact that my parents were much bigger than me was of much greater consequence than the fact that most of the other kids my size had darker skin.

I even felt culturally more similar to my darker-hued peers than to the previous generations of my own family. For one, I didn't talk like my parents, who had migrated to New York from Pennsylvania and Connecticut. I spoke like the other kids in the neighborhood. On the playground everyone pretty much spoke the same language with the same unique accent, no matter where our parents came from. While adults might speak only Spanish, or talk with a heavy drawl if they came from down South, our way of talking was like a layered cake; it had many distinctly rich flavors, but in our mouths they all got mixed up together. When we "snapped" on each other, little did we know we were using the same ironic lilt and intonation once employed in the Jewish shtetls of Central Europe. This Yiddish-like English had mixed with influences from southern Italians, Irish, and other immigrant groups to form the basic New Yorkese of the mid-twentieth century. We spoke with open vowels and dropped our rs: *quarter* was *quartah*, and *water* was *watah*. To this European stew we added the Southern tendency to cut off the endings of some words—*runnin', skippin', jumpin'*—a habit that came northward with many blacks during the Great Migration. We also turned our *t*s into *d*s, as in "Lemme get *fiddy* cents." The latest and most powerful influence was Puerto Rican. Within the Spanish-speaking world, Puerto Ricans were notorious for their lazy *r*s, just as New Yorkers were, so the fit was perfect. Whenever someone said *mira*, the Spanish term for *look*, it came out *media*.

Although Spanish separated the native speakers from those of us who picked it up on the playground, the presence of the large Puerto Rican population had the opposite effect for me, narrowing the racial rift between others and myself. Their various hues of tan and brown made my looks seem a matter of degree rather than of kind, filling in the spectrum of color separating most of the black kids from me. It helped that I was not entirely pale. My hair was as dark as that of anyone around. If studied closely, my eyes betrayed brown shades around the interior of the iris, fanning out to green, but from afar they looked no lighter than those of a lot of the kids. My skin tone ranged from white to brownish depending on the time of year. For all these reasons, I perceived skin color in particular and race in general as something mutable, something that could change with the seasons or with an extended trip back to Puerto Rico. In this I was no different from scholars two centuries earlier who described "blackness" as a universal freckle that would fade with time spent in the North or darken over the course of generations in Africa.

While I may have been oblivious to race as a toddler, I certainly recognized gender differences. More than anything else, I prayed for the baby to be a girl. As it turned out, I got my wish.

How did I, the child of two white artists, end up living in the inner city—in the projects of 1969, no less? The short answer is that we had no money. My mother liked to joke that she had to "lie up" about our income to get food stamps. My father worked part-time in an art supply store; my mother was a graduate student at Empire State College. Despite our family's economic circumstances, we enjoyed a degree of choice about where to live. My parents could have moved to a white, working-class neighborhood in the outer boroughs or in New Jersey, for example. Our neighbors, by contrast, were largely unwelcome elsewhere for reasons of race and financial status. It was this modicum of choice, not skin color per se, that ultimately distinguished us from our neighbors.

The long answer of how we ended up there lay in the same tabloid paper that my mother scanned each morning with her Bustello coffee, searching for news of local murders and rapes of the day before. It was through an advertisement in the *Daily News* that we all ended up living in the Masaryk Towers complex just south of Avenue D in Manhattan. In 1968, my parents were living a few blocks north of the projects, in a tenement apartment that had been broken into so many times they had to chain their black-and-white television to the radiator. But that didn't protect them from one particular burglar. By chance, my mother was standing outside the building and looked up to see him climb through her window from the fire escape. She ran to the corner and called the police, who arrived just as the crook came downstairs, his arms piled up with whatever he thought he could sell. The cops threw him up against the wall, then took him down to the Tombs, where they held suspects to be arraigned. It turned out that the guy was a junkie with seven prior arrests, but he still managed to plea-bargain the charges from attempted robbery down to loitering. The judge gave him two weeks at Riker's Island—two days, apparently, for each prior.

Jonesing from a lack of drugs and facing the prospect of going cold turkey for two weeks in jail, he vented his anger at my mother as the bailiff dragged him out of the courtroom. "Lady," he said, running his shackled hands through his stringy blond hair, "when I get out, I'm going to get you." He wiped his runny nose onto the hair of his thick, tattooed arm and added: "I know where you live, so I'm going to find you, and then I'm going to kill you." He spoke these menacing words eloquently, as if he were preaching.

Whenever asked why we ended up in Masaryk Towers, my mother would tell this story, describing every detail of the burglar's appearance, tone, and demeanor. Even when I was just a few years old, I could sense her guilt at having moved the family to an unsafe neighborhood—and perhaps for having taken an apartment slot from some more deserving family. She told this story to reassure herself that the family had no choice and had to act quickly, even if that wasn't 100 percent true.

As the family lore goes, my parents had been talking about renovating a loft in Soho. They had one already picked out, a 3,000-square-foot walkup in an iron-clad building on Spring Street. The loft was selling for a few thousand dollars, since it was completely raw space, but even that was beyond my parents' means. They might have been able to borrow the down payment from my mother's parents, but they certainly never would have qualified for a loan for the repairs necessary to make it livable. Besides, my grandparents shared an ideology against overt financial transfers to family members. My grandfather used to joke with my sister that he would buy her a car when she graduated from college, any model she wanted. This raised her suspicions, so she asked, "What about Dalton; will you buy him a car, too?"

"No," he answered. "I might still be alive when his comes due, but I won't be by the time you finish school."

At this my sister crossed her arms and pouted, upset at his calculations and at the fact that he planned on dying. As it turns out, he wouldn't have had to make good on a promise to me, either; shortly before I finished college he died in a freak golfing accident in which a friend ran him over with a cart.

My grandparents' relative wealth served an indirect—but important—role for my sister and me growing up: We had a security blanket in the event of a major catastrophe. Needless to say, this was another important but silent way in which my family differed from others in the neighborhood.

In retrospect, I'm sure my parents could have bought the loft had they really wanted to, but for some reason they didn't. Maybe they were averse to the risk involved, or to the work that the renovation would have required at a time when they wanted to focus on their careers; maybe it was something more insidious, a form of inertia that prevents people from moving up the class ladder. Whenever I asked either parent, I got the same story about the menacing burglar and the need to move quickly. Each used to tell this story in a strange tone falling somewhere between giddiness and sarcasm, sounding wistful and defensive, like a boxer who missed his only chance at a title fight. They spoke of it as if it were someone else's life.

Whatever the reason, the choice had been made, and its consequences cascaded over the rest of my childhood. It meant the difference between living in a good school district and living in a bad one, between having our own rooms and sharing a bunk bed, between having a study for my mother's writing career and her working out of a closet, between having and not having a painting space for my father. Such seemingly small decisions can make the difference between rich and poor, but scientists will never be able to capture their effects in statistics. Today that loft is worth millions, and my sister and I make a sport out of grumbling at our parents over the missed opportunity.

Instead of renovating the postindustrial space, they answered an advertisement in the *Daily News* soliciting applications for a newly minted, federally supported housing complex not far from their tenement. They went to look at the place. The entire stretch of Avenue D from Fourteenth Street to well below Houston Street—almost a mile long—was lined with projects. Every few blocks the brown-bricked dwellings changed in name and only slightly in style. The Jacob Riis houses melted into the Lillian Walds and then the Bernard Baruchs, names that held little meaning for most of the residents of these complexes. One structure might be a story or two taller than the adjacent one or have bricks a shade darker, but otherwise the buildings looked exactly alike, and they remained the same over the course of decades. Man landed on the moon, the oil shock of 1973 came and went, business cycles rolled by, but nothing about the projects gave any sign of societal or economic change. There was never any new construction or renovation. And since the buildings were brick, there was never even a new coat of paint. The projects constituted a static monument to the social policy of their time.

Each group of buildings took up two or three city blocks. One cluster of houses was aligned parallel to Avenue D; the next set of buildings pointed its corners outward toward the street. My father said he liked the atmosphere; the brown building patterns reminded him of his multilayered acrylic paintings. By contrast, my mother's spirits were sagging. Just a few years earlier, when she had moved to New York from Pennsylvania, people had planted flowers in boxes on their window ledges all across the Lower East Side. The bright colors and odor of petunias had attracted her like a hummingbird.

The "flower box movement" had been the most urban manifestation of 1960s flower power, but by the end of the decade all that remained were broken pieces of clay pots on the ledges of the Avenue D tenements. I don't know why the flowers didn't keep—maybe because the residents had more important struggles to worry about, bigger battles to fight.

When my parents arrived at Masaryk Towers to apply for housing, they were told the new complex was different from the other projects in the area. Masaryk Towers represented an attempt to integrate the working class with the non-working class through a New York State Housing and Community Renewal program called Mitchell-Lama. The housing complex had its own security force, was funded by its own government grant, and was managed by a nonprofit corporation instead of the city, all of which my mother found encouraging. Little did she know the security guards would not do much to stop the violence in our buildings—cops getting shot in the elevator, hostages being taken in the pharmacy, girls getting raped in the stairwell. After all, even though Masaryk had certain amenities, it was sandwiched between two city-managed projects in much worse condition. At the time my mother was impressed with the layout. The six buildings surrounded a central courtyard area and housed several thousand people—a population rivaling that of the coal-mining town she had grown up in, compressed into the square footage of two city blocks. The courtyard held three small playgrounds, roughly divided by age appropriateness, as well as trees and grass and wildlife ranging from the tropical—huge cockroaches and water bugs—to the temperate, in the form of thick-furred squirrels. It was springtime; the trees were lush with white blossoms, and the grass was thick. To my mother the grass seemed greener than any she had ever seen; but maybe that was only in contrast to the hot, glass-littered concrete that covered the rest of the neighborhood.

"It's just like Penn State," Ellen said, nostalgic for her college as she tugged on my father's arm. She had selected her university based on how pretty it was, and now she would do the same for her family's residence.

Once inside the buildings, however, my father balked, thinking the clean lines and low ceilings of the cookie-cutter apartments the urban equivalent of some tract-housing development on Long Island. To him, being an artist in New York meant living in a prewar walkup, a railroad apartment with cracked plaster, layers of lead paint, and a leaky faucet. Moving into one of these towering buildings was in his mind like moving out of the city; the place was too bourgeois for him, too suburban. But it was this very sense of country living within the city limits that appealed to my mother. They landed an apartment on the top, twenty-first floor—the "ghetto penthouse," my sister and I later called it, unaware of the tastelessness of our moniker. We could see the hills of New Jersey from one window, the farthest reaches of Queens from the other, and enjoyed a river-to-river view of the Manhattan skyline. If we didn't look straight down at the burned-out, boarded-up slums and the periodic fires that produced them, we could imagine that we lived in a middle-class high-rise in the heart of New York City.

So in 1968 my father and mother moved in, toting their scanty load of furniture and personal belongings in a friend's van. I was born the following year. Shortly after that, I almost died. At three weeks of age, I contracted spinal meningitis, a rare infection that inflames the lining of the brain and spinal cord. The disease manifested itself on perhaps the worst day of the year: the Fourth of July, which not only is a major holiday, leaving hospitals staffed by skeleton crews, but also falls just two weeks after the new crop of medical residents has rotated in. I spent my first Independence Day being prodded and poked and spinal-tapped by amateurish hands. I was put on an antibiotic IV, but nothing seemed to work. I was getting sicker and sicker, suffering from backbreaking convulsions by the hour and passing stool the crumbly texture of dried-out clay. My weight dropped precipitously.

"The antibiotics are obviously not working!" my mother screamed at the resident who was tending to me.

"Don't worry, madam," said the resident. "The results of the spinal tap will be back shortly. Don't you worry now."

Ellen knew better, having worked in a hospital microbiology lab. The spinal fluid would sit in the in-box for the entire holiday weekend, and I would be dead by the time it was cultured. So she broke into the lab. Sure enough, it was completely empty. She didn't turn on the lights for fear of being discovered. She ran the assay herself and scribbled the results on a notepad. I wonder what would have happened had my mother not been white. No one questioned her as she rushed around the hallways—but a frantic black or Hispanic woman might have drawn greater scrutiny.

The results of my mother's test showed that I was suffering from a rare type of infection that was unresponsive to the medication they had been giving me, which treated only the common strain. My mother sent the results up under separate cover, then rushed in to find the doctor calmly changing his prescription. "You see," he told her, "I told you there was nothing to worry about, madam. I see here that we need to switch to a gram-negative antibiotic."

Still, I got worse before I got better.

"Why don't you consider adopting Alfonso here?" the doctor suggested on one of my worse days. Alfonso was a healthy Puerto Rican infant whose mother had abandoned him to the hospital ward. Ellen didn't appreciate the suggestion that I was dying; she rushed at the well-meaning doctor with clenched teeth and fists before my father restrained her. But my parents grew to like Alfonso, with his hoarse voice and black hair that stood straight up, and as I rallied they even discussed the topic of adopting him—as a brother, not a replacement for me, they were always quick to add.

As it turned out, my parents never had to face that issue. A month later I got a clean bill of health from a neurologist, who tossed me around like a football to test my Moro reflex. When I splayed my arms out, flailing in mid-air, he made his diagnosis: "No detectable brain damage, he's good to go." Still, I was frail and needy, and my parents had their hands full when I came home. They continued to visit Alfonso for a little while, but taking care of a convalescing baby entailed so much work and lack of sleep that they scrapped any notion of adopting another child. My parents eventually lost track of Alfonso; he disappeared into the world of foster care. I sometimes wonder what became of my almost-brother, with a tinge of guilt over the random good fortune of my recovery.

After my stint in the hospital, we paid a summer visit to my grandparents in Pennsylvania, stopping at the Woodstock festival on our way back. By the time I finally arrived in our neighborhood for good, the fifteen-year-old Oldsmobile we had been given by my mother's parents was shot. It overheated twice on the Henry Hudson Parkway, and we rolled into town with steam seeping from under the hood and profanities spewing from my father's lips. We cruised past the rows of blighted buildings that lined Avenue D, their fire escapes hanging like sculpture. Flocks of pet pigeons circled overhead, and a skinny teenager was climbing the Houston Street traffic pole to retrieve a pair of basketball sneakers that had been hanging there like a piñata for over a year. He snagged the sneakers and shimmied down the pole, the shoes dangling from his teeth; his Afro hairstyle made his head look extraterrestrially huge from a distance. Little did I know it, but I was about to spend my first year as a white minority, a honky in a community of color. It was the beginning of my life and the end of the 1960s.

The flower box movement had embodied the notion that poverty was primarily an aesthetic problem. If we could just spruce things up a bit, we'd all have more hope; we might even become middle class. But by 1968 every surface in our neighborhood was covered with graffiti. Big Cyrillic-looking letters proclaimed DKA (*Damien Kicks Ass*) or asked SWN (*Say What Nigger?*). If a critic got to the letters they might have "Toy" scribbled over them, the ultimate dis of a tag. The text was judged not only on content but also on the style in which it was drawn and, perhaps most important, on its location. If it were tagged somewhere hard to get to, it was unlikely a rival would be able to tag over it. Under the overhang of the Williamsburg Bridge was one particularly daring spot. Even the walls of the projects eighteen stories off the ground displayed the occasional tag, when someone was inventive and fearless enough to rig up a way of dangling out the window and scrolling over the brown or yellow bricks that made up our world. Perhaps because they were the most visible marker of urban blight, graffiti scrawlings, more than crime or drugs or family breakup, were what embarrassed me when I brought friends home from other areas of the city. It was four-color, in-your-face poverty.

Anything that passed through our neighborhood got covered in graffiti, especially the buses that connected us to the rest of Manhattan. Every vehicle on the M14 line was awash in paint and markers, alternately bright and fading, spelling out messages of identity that were only legible to those in the know. Each tag was a warning or a welcome, encoded with special messages that we read daily, as we might editorials. To the passengers who boarded over in the numbered avenues on the West Side, the overinflated letters that arched and swelled across the corrugated metal sides of the buses must have seemed like gibberish; the only message they carried was a warning to stay out of the "bad" neighborhood.

Then there were the colorful murals dedicated to overdose victims. "Te amo José," read the biggest and brightest painting, which depicted a big syringe dripping blood and José with a goatee on his chin and a halo about his head—half devil, half angel. Out of respect no one ever tagged over the murals; they were the only surfaces in the neighborhood that weren't covered in the chaos of magic markers and spray paint.

The M14 bus started at Delancey Street and headed straight north, passing all the projects on its way to the Con Edison plant that marked the border of the Lower East Side at Fourteenth Street. The electric utility was the most exotic structure that any of us had encountered, so it was fitting that it sat at Fourteenth Street, on the upper lip of the neighborhood, intimating things unknown that lay west and north of it. The power plant occupied a series of city blocks and consisted of strange-looking coils that seemed like props from a Frankenstein movie. Though we kids looked studiously for some sign of electricity being produced, the huge capacitors and transformers made no sound, gave no hint of any activity. Workmen never seemed to enter or leave the huge compound; there didn't even seem to be entrances. The only sign of life was the smoke that puffed from the triumvirate of chimneys that crowned the main building. Those primitive plumes of steam seemed incongruous next to the complicated electrical devices at street level. I spent years trying to detect patterns in the white vapor, marking when it streamed out continuously, when it formed distinct little cloudlike balls, and when the beast was entirely breathless. But if there was some message in the utility's smoke signals, I could not decipher its language. In its impersonal operation, the Con Edison plant provided a too-perfect metaphor for the institutions of society that both ran our community and demarcated it from the rest of the world.

Across from the Avenue D projects stood another manifestation of poverty: the slums. It was as if some social scientist had constructed a very crude experiment, randomly assigning people with low socioeconomic status to live on one side of the street or the other. But the project/slum experiment would have yielded no conclusions, for those who lived in the projects were no better off than those who lived in the rundown apartments across the street. We were all on food stamps; some of us were on welfare; others worked. It made no difference. There was no particular stigma to living in the projects as compared to right next door to them.

While the projects cast an oppressive shadow over Avenue D, the tenements brimmed over with street life. Though many of them were condemned or boarded up, often burned down for insurance money by the landlords themselves, almost every building that still functioned as a residence—and even some that did not—enjoyed an active storefront. Men sat in front of these bodegas and restaurants playing dominos, while children ran to and fro in front of them, their mothers sitting on the hoods of cars or rocking infants on their hips. When it was hot, locals would open the fire hydrants so kids could take turns ducking into the forceful stream. Back then the fire department had not issued caps that allowed for moderate water flows, so the city fought a constant battle with overheated residents. Every so often a fireman showed up and turned off the water, but it would only stay off for half an hour or so; then someone with the special wrench would open the flow again.

Kids seemed to roam freely, but in reality everyone watched everyone else's children; there was a degree of community-based social control that would not have been obvious to the casual observer. The same can be said for the traffic. Drivers seemed to disobey most parking restrictions, motoring freely up and down the avenue, following their own logic much as the children did; yet traffic jams were hardly ever a problem. Men washed their cars with buckets of soapy water that came from the same gushing hydrants the kids played in. Others kept all four doors and the trunk open to blast salsa music to the whole block. During summer the entire neighborhood seemed to be partying all the time. In winter it went dormant and receded into the apartments, which served as spores to preserve social relations until the next spring.

When viewed over a longer historical trajectory, it might not be so surprising that my parents ended up raising their family where they did. Each took a different route to arrive at Columbia Street in 1968. My mother's ancestors had once passed through this very same neighborhood, long before there were any projects or flower boxes. These Hungarian immigrants rolled cigars for a living until one of them saved up enough money to leave the Lower East Side for Susquehanna County, Pennsylvania. Whenever someone asked my mother how her family ended up there, she merely said, "That's where the horse died." It served as an explanation, but in actuality she had no idea why her grandparents settled in Carbondale, a small coal-mining town in the northeastern part of the state.

For my mother's family there was no such thing as class, but they did harbor some primordial notion of race. To them the world was divided into two racial categories: Jewish and other. Each small town in the Alleghenies was typically home to two Jewish families, the doctor's and the dry-goods shopkeeper's. Converging two by two at one or another's home to play bridge or mahjong, the members of this diaspora felt comfortable enough among themselves to brag about their children or tell ribald jokes about Jesus and Moses playing golf. Among the *goyim*, however, they merely nodded politely and tried to go relatively unnoticed. During World War II my grandfather tried to enlist in the infantry but was turned down because he was deaf in one ear, so instead he practiced dentistry for the army. He and my grandmother also took in a German refugee who had been orphaned in the Holocaust.

Martin, the German kid, was as confused as a Jewish five-year-old could be. When Hitler's voice came across the BBC, he'd stand up and salute like a well-trained SS officer. My mother's brother would instruct, "No, Hitler bad," and spit on the ground, then look skyward and declare: "Roosevelt good." To no avail. When he wasn't yelling "Heil Hitler" or waking up from nightmares, Martin was eating. He ate as if the food would be taken away from him at any moment. Evidently I ate the same way, since each time I gulped down food that was meant to be chewed I was called "Martin" and scolded for my manners. My grandparents and mother described his method of eating to me many times: He would crane his sinewy neck over the table and lift the plate to his lips, shoveling as fast as he could with a hand cupped to form a human backhoe.

After several months Martin finally got permanent placement with a couple who had no children of their own. My mother and grandparents were relieved to see him go, though they would never have admitted this to anyone outside their Jewish circle. Among other Jews they could laugh about Martin and his pro-Nazi sympathies, but among their non-Jewish neighbors they would never allow it to be spoken of. Even those of my mother's more secular generation were less open with the

Poles and Italians who populated the coal-mining towns than with each other. It didn't matter how much money anyone had; all that mattered was whether they were Jewish or goy.

In the mid-1950s my mother went off to Penn State and was greeted in her crinoline and poodle skirt by President Eisenhower, whose brother was the university president. Everyone signed in and out of the dormitories and obeyed the weekday eight o'clock curfew. Feet were kept on the floor at all times in the dormitory parlor rooms, and all the boys and girls kissed goodnight in unison at the end of their Friday or Saturday night dates when the chimes struck one a.m.

But by the time Ellen left Penn State the 1960s had begun. There was no need for the tradition of dormitory panty raids; couples were shacking up off campus, and gays were coming out of the closet. However, the few blacks who attended the university still kept to themselves; after all, the state of Pennsylvania ranked among the highest in Ku Klux Klan membership. When students organized a picket to protest a local barbershop's refusal to serve black customers, only whites marched, my mother among them. The protest succeeded and made the news, drawing some CORE organizers to town. At that time Jews and blacks were allies in the "cause," so the nationwide group drafted my mother to head up its new campus branch. A week later boxes and boxes of leaflets arrived at her dorm room. But she had more intellectual sympathy than grassroots energy, so the cartons sat gathering dust.

After graduation she moved first to Philadelphia and then to New York City's Greenwich Village. There she picked up where she had left off in college, joining a civil rights group in the hope of gathering material for her writing career. In the summer of 1964 she attended a training seminar sponsored by the Student Nonviolent Coordinating Committee (SNCC). It was held in the dingy basement of a large, Moorish-style building that resembled a Masonic shrine, deep in the heart of Brooklyn. My mother and about three others were placed in a line for their indoctrination. In the darkened room, veteran lunch-counter integrators played the role of Southern bigots in order to train the new recruits in the art of passive resistance. First one of the leaders warned them against wearing ties or jewelry, yanking on their earrings and neckties for emphasis. Then my mother and the other neophytes were handed placards and told to march in a circle while the trainers harassed them. Some people really got into their roles—especially the black members.

"Get the fuck out of our county, you goddamn nigger lover!" screamed one black man.

"Do you like niggers?" my mother remembers being yelled at. "I bet you like to fuck niggers with those big tits of yours!"

Unnerved, my mother was about to call it quits, but within moments the veterans had broken roles and stood around smoking cigarettes, congratulating each other on their respective performances. When the rush of fear had finally dissipated and she had caught her breath, my mother volunteered for her first Freedom Ride.

Initially my mother's integrated carload didn't encounter much resistance as they made their way through Virginia. Her main worry was how much weight she was putting on; the protesters were eating about eight meals a day. Most of the restaurant staff made them wait a while and didn't smile or make eye contact, but they served them food just the same. The protesters never got poisoned, as they were warned might happen. Only once did they encounter strong resistance, sitting in a North Carolina diner for several hours as the proprietor and his staff ignored them. As time elapsed, a crowd gathered outside, mostly men, wielding bottles and clubs. My mother was scared for the first time since the training session.

Finally, just as the sun was setting, gigantic state troopers made taller by imposing hats and boots stormed into the establishment. One of them announced, "You're not welcome here." He signaled to the rest of the troopers, who dragged the members of the group out one after another. As my mother tells the story with a laugh, she was so relieved to leave the restaurant that she went even more limp than she had been trained to. The Freedom Riders weren't charged but were informally exiled from the county. That night, as they were leaving in their borrowed car, tired, hungry, and grumpy, a fleet of vehicles pulled up beside them on the highway. In the moonlight, my mother could see the glint of rifles and shotguns sticking out of cracked-open windows. One car rammed into them, trying to run them off the road and into the tobacco fields, but they kept going. When they finally drove across the county line, the swarm of cars fell off their tail one by one, like a fighter plane squadron on an aborted attack mission.

That ended my mother's career as a civil rights activist.

Next she served a stint as a medical volunteer in Haiti. There she got her first taste of how it felt to be a white minority. In the poorest country in the Western Hemisphere, she worked for one of the richest men in the world, Dr. Larremar Mellon of the Pittsburgh steel family. Mellon had once been a playboy who wore a top hat and puffed on a long ivory cigarette holder. However, after meeting Albert Schweitzer, he gave up his hedonistic life and, at the age of forty-five, went to medical school. He and his wife later founded the Hôpital Albert Schweitzer, which tried to meet the medical needs of the population of Port-au-Prince.

My mother had studied for two years at Jefferson Medical School in Philadelphia as a nondegree "special" student, since women were not yet eligible for medical degrees there. She finally gave up her efforts to become a doctor, but the training served her well in Haiti. There she ran the lab, culturing all the blood and other samples taken from malnourished patients who showed signs of infection. She would read the culture and dispense the appropriate antibiotic. Most of the diseases were caused by *E. coli*, since people drank, cooked, and washed with the same water supply they used as a latrine.

Though Haiti was one of the most class-conscious nations in the Western Hemisphere, the concept was lost on my mother. While there she met many of the local elite, including Jacques Saint-Bris, who sold her a painting for five dollars. A few years later he was "discovered" and gained worldwide renown for his application of classical European techniques to the depiction of local voodoo culture. By that time the painting my mother had bought, a brightly colored abstract that resembled a pea-cock if it resembled anything, had ballooned in value to the point that it was by far the most precious thing my parents owned—the only instance in which they were able to cash in on some of their cultural capital. The painting sat in the dark-ness of a closet getting a water stain, while the voodoo dolls from the Port-au-Prince Iron Market stood proudly like face-less soldiers on the edges of our bookshelves.

After returning from the Caribbean, my mother spent the rest of the 1960s wandering the streets of New York in search of inspiration for her short stories, oblivious to the social and physical dangers that lurked around her. She wore the flowery dresses popular at the time, her curly black hair braided into long pigtails that frayed like twine. She had the same oval face and long features she would bequeath to her children, and she wore round eyeglasses that slipped a third of the way down her nose until their momentum was stopped by a Semitic bump on an otherwise aquiline feature. They hung there sort of ele-gantly, and her big, dark eyes peered over their upper rims, so that she always looked as if she were reading something, even while walking or talking. Often she wore mismatched socks underneath her sandals. She didn't need any drugs to keep up with the quirkiness of the time; her mind generated enough random disturbances on its own. Once she glimpsed a sign over the top of her glasses and thought it read, "Dancing Men Above." She stopped, excited at the prospect of a free show. But the sign read "Danger Men Above," which she realized only after her neck had cramped up from craning skyward.

My mother's misreading of signs was not limited to text. Frequently she got quite involved with men before they would confess to her that they were gay. Many of these ersatz romances evolved into lifelong friendships, with my mother often playing the part of stand-in fiancée for the benefit of a gay friend's unsuspecting parents. She was as oblivious to sexual orientation as she was to class and status; these concepts simply didn't register with her.

By contrast, my father, Steve, was steeped in class but had no concept of race. He perceived subtle distinctions in manner and style and drew from them the finest class gradations. But on the subject of race and out-groups, he was as oblivious as Ellen was walking the streets of New York. His mother came from an old New England family that traced its roots back through Roger Williams and Miles Standish to the Mayflower, though no one would guess as much from her constant stream of profanities. She made a career of flaunting class lines. Her real name was Hazel Hatch, but she forbade anyone to call her that. Instead she went by Tiz. As soon as Prohibition took effect, she started drinking and smoking and cursing. When the Daughters of the American Revolution asked her to sign on, she told them they weren't good enough for her, that she could be a member of the Colonial Dames, who had descended not just from soldiers of the Revolution but from *officers* in that war. Of course, when the Colonial Dames came calling, she told them to go to hell. She married a philandering Irish business executive. Always independent, she worked during her two pregnancies and while raising her children, never retiring until she became terminally ill. She spent much of her married life in one of the oldest houses in the state of Connecticut, but she died impoverished in a trailer park.

Steve's father, Walter, was a social climber who had moved to the Northeast from Ohio. He had smooth skin, stunningly high cheekbones, and a full head of hair until the day he dropped dead from a heart attack. A vice president at Burlington Mills, he was one of the first persons to commute daily between Connecticut and New York City, making it easier to conceal his extramarital arrangements. Often he would call in from the city, telling his family that he would be working late and staying at his pied-à-terre. They knew better and resented him for it. Late one night he was driving along the Connecticut Turnpike when a drunken hobo stepped out in front of his car. He struck the man and instantly killed him. It was a clash of classes. Walter, who had spent his entire life cultivating his taste in clothes, books, and women, plowed into a man who had none of the above and not a cent to his name. This incident always came to mind first whenever I thought of my grandfather—perhaps because it intrigued me that he actually killed someone, or perhaps because I wondered how he got away with it.

Although my grandfather had gotten to his position without the benefit of much formal schooling—a feat that was still possible in his generation—he was obsessed with education. He sent my father to prep schools in Boston and New York, where young Steve suffered from a case of acne so severe that a family friend wanted to cite him in a dermatology textbook he authored. Whenever he talked about his teenage complexion or the experimental surgery he underwent to sandblast his face, my father would rub the scar tissue that resulted, talking about the experience like a tough war veteran who was proud just to have survived the whole ordeal.

Though he was a star football player for Brown and Nichols Academy, his acne separated him from the rest of the prep-school boys. Maybe this explains why he broke ranks with his classmates, most of whom enrolled in the elite colleges of the Northeast, to study painting at Lawrence College, a small liberal arts school in Appleton, Wisconsin. When Steve was a junior there, his father was forced from his position at Burlington Mills in the type of hostile takeover that would not become commonplace for another quarter-century. My grandfather took it as an opportunity to go into business for himself. He started a series of companies that sold products such as vertical blinds; but these goods, like the corporate raid that had made him an entrepreneur in the first place, were ahead of their time. His businesses went under, and his family lost its landmark 1664 home. Steve had to drop out of college for lack of funds.

Every family that experiences a socioeconomic setback must come up with its own narrative of why it happened; ours was "Too far ahead of his time." We worked on this rationale, this excuse, telling and retelling Walter's story to hone its details and to forgive ourselves for being guilty of that ultimate sin in American society: downward mobility.

When he ran out of money for school, Steve went to New

York to make it as an abstract painter, following in the footsteps of his heroes, Jackson Pollock and Willem de Kooning. He loved bebop and had a well-worn copy of Jack Kerouac's *On the Road*, but I could never imagine him as a beatnik, and he denies ever having dressed or acted the part. In New York he worked at many low-wage jobs, ranging from stock boy at a paint supply store to "assembly-line" artist to canvas remover. The last job entailed removing canvases from frames and peeling away the first, painted layer of canvas. These oil paintings were meticulously hand-brushed by South Koreans. The painters worked for pennies in their devastated postwar economy. Perhaps because they knew their works were destined for the United States, they primarily depicted American GIs. As seen by the Korean artists, the soldiers had huge, round eyes; some were crying equally huge, round tears, which splashed onto their combat boots as they stared longingly at the viewer with homesickness. My father's job for eight hours a day was to shear off these paintings in order to reveal the clean, virgin canvas underneath. Evidently art could be imported duty-free, while raw canvas and frames could not. It was cheaper for the distributor to waste a whole layer of canvas and oil paints, along with the labor of these Korean workers, than to pay the import taxes for the blank canvas and frame. This was my father's first lesson on the value of art and artists in the modern economy. Before that job ended, he sneaked a small GI portrait home under his jacket. *Vince*, as it was captioned, hung in the hallway of our apartment for many years, reminding us of a different kind of poverty from the one we saw around us.

Steve continued his mother's class rebellion. He spent most of his days painting, trading work with other artists, and studying the *Racing Form*. He shared a small, inexpensive studio in Chinatown with a couple of artists, one of whom—to my fascination and delight—painted only triangles. My father's clothes and hands were always splattered with paint, which embarrassed me to no end whenever he picked me up from school or a friend's house. Anytime he got some extra money he hopped the A-train to Aqueduct Racetrack—which he called the "horsie zoo" to trick my sister and me into coming along when it was his turn to take care of us. He spent hours studying the odds on the huge tote board, scribbling numbers onto a notepad or banging them into a plastic calculator. As he handicapped each race, he rubbed the yellowed scar tissue on his cheeks, the fossilized record of his prep school suffering. Partly because of these unchanging calluses, the signs of age always seemed missing from his body. He never grayed much over the course of his life. He had a benign balding spot on the top of his head that always stayed the size of a half-dollar, never growing in area or severity. He seemed to lose fat and gain muscle over the course of his adult life. He was as oblivious to his own age as he was to the flow of bettors around him: old Jewish men chewing on cigar stubs, young Rastafarians with two-foot-high hair smoking spliffs, Chinese retirees hocking lugies onto the ticket-littered floor. All he saw were the numbers in the *Racing Form*. His obliviousness was the opposite of my mother's: whereas she was prone to see things that weren't there, he was likely not to notice things that were. Both adaptations would serve them well in the inner city, where my mother maintained a vigilant and healthy dose of paranoia and where my father often had to step over unconscious junkies splayed out in the street or ignore bleating sirens as he walked my sister and me to and from school each day.

Learning race is like learning a language. First we try mouthing all sounds. Then we learn which are not words and which have meaning to the people around us. Likewise, for my sister and me, the first step in our socialization was being taught that we weren't black. Like a couple of boot camp trainees, we had first to be stripped of any illusions we harbored of being like the other kids, then be built back up in whiteness.

My sister Alexandra started getting the message as early as age two. She and I attended nursery school courtesy of the federally subsidized Head Start program. One of the Great Society initiatives that seemed to parallel our lives, Head Start was the result of a decade of research showing that the educational deficits poor kids faced in high school could be traced back to their preschool years—that is, to the time when they were with their parents at home. Never mind what this implied about certain people's parenting practices; the answer was to provide poor kids with day care where they would get at least one nutritious meal a day and be exposed to educational toys. Head Start even had a government-mandated commencement day to get us accustomed to the idea of graduating so it wouldn't seem strange by the time we reached high school. We had to make our own caps and gowns out of crepe paper.

Despite the nominal separation of church and state, our local program first met in the basement of a local church before moving to the community center of the Bernard Baruch houses on the other side of Columbia Street. Likewise, our Head Start celebrated all Christian holidays. Each December Santa Claus came bounding in with a bag of presents and a series of "Ho! Ho! Hos!" so enthusiastic and deep in tone that they scared us and shook the cubbyholes where we stored our things each morning. Then he would sit down and balance each kid on his knee as if he were the ventriloquist and we the wooden dummies.

"And have you been a naughty girl or a nice girl?" he asked my sister when her turn came one particular year.

"I want a Big Wheel," she responded, her manner as rehearsed as Santa's.

It didn't matter what they asked for; everyone got dolls. The boys got boy dolls, and the girls got girl dolls. In line with the consciousness of the times, the teachers had made sure that the dolls were ethnically appropriate. The other kids' dolls looked like black versions of Ken and Barbie, while my sister ended up with the only white doll in her class. All the figures were generic knockoffs, probably bought from a street vendor in Chinatown; in fact, the black dolls looked exactly like the white one, but with a coat of brown paint on their bodies and hair. Nonetheless, when the other kids saw that Alexandra had a *real* Barbie, they stampeded her, begging, pleading, and demanding that she trade with them. She clutched the doll to her chest as girls and even boys tried to pry it from her.

"Black is beautiful!" the teachers screamed over the din of crying and yelling.

"We want Barbie!" the kids yelled back in unison.

Finally, one kid pulled hard at the white doll's legs and broke the toy in half. Evidently satisfied that she had secured at least a piece of Barbie, she scurried off to a corner to dress up the half-doll. Eventually my sister got the other half back and willingly traded her white doll for one in the black style. She was content. All she wanted was a doll with long hair that she could comb.

At some point that same week, our grandparents called to wish us a Happy Chanukah. My sister recounted the Barbie events to my grandmother, who, in turn, told her the story of King Solomon and the baby. "Two women each said that the baby was hers," she explained slowly, enunciating each syllable to my sister who, at that stage in her development, paid eager attention to anything involving babies. "King Solomon told them that he would cut the baby in half and then each could have part of it." She explained that one of the women broke down crying, offering the baby to the other woman. " 'You are the true mother,' the King told this one," Grandma recounted as our grandfather breathed not quite silently on the other phone extension, as was his custom.

"Do you know how he knew?" Grandma then asked, trying to pry the moral of the story out of Alexandra. "What would you say if King Solomon said that to you about your baby?"

"I would take the top half," my sister explained. "So I could brush her hair."

In the family annals, my sister's answer to the King Solomon question was what got told and retold; the issue of black beauty, the other kids' desperation for the white doll, and the idea that a "real" Barbie could only be white was left for the parents of the other children to sort out. It wasn't our problem; after all, we *were* the color of Barbie.

The next year everyone got black dolls whether they liked it or not. And since they had long hair, my sister was happy.

By the time she was six years old, Alexandra had tired of combing and brushing and wanted to do more advanced hair things. All her friends now had cornrows, and my sister begged my mother to braid some for her, too. Alexandra's best friend, Adoonie, lived in the building across from ours in the complex. She and my sister spent hours envying each other's hair. Adoonie wanted blonde locks that looked like Farrah Fawcett's, while my sister wanted the cornrows that made Adoonie fit in with the rest of the kids in the playground. My sister got particularly jealous each month when Adoonie and her mother unbraided and cleaned her cornrows with witch hazel, then rebraided them so neatly that they looked like rows of stitches on some machine-knitted sweater. The whole procedure took hours, and since Adoonie was an only child she and her mother could spend an entire leisurely day on the endeavor. It was pure mother-daughter time, something Alexandra craved in the face of her competition with me for parental attention.

"Please, can you do my hair like Doonie's?" she'd plead with our mother every so often, trying to braid her own hair to demonstrate the technique. "Please, please, please!" My mother, who couldn't draw, knit, or cornrow a straight line, told Alexandra that her hair type wouldn't work for that style but was beautiful in its own right.

"I don't care; I want my hair like Doonie's—like everybody's," Alexandra pouted. Ellen wiped the tears from her face and spent a good portion of the next hour brushing my sister's hair in the mirror. After a couple more episodes like this one, Alexandra finally let go of the dream of cornrows. But the next year the movie *10* came out, making Bo Derek famous. At first all the little girls thought Bo Derek, with her cornrowed hair and tropical tan, must be black. They wanted to grow their own cornrows longer so that they, like Bo Derek, could have the best of both worlds: long hair and tight braids along their scalp.

Then one of the older girls told the group that Bo Derek was actually white, a revelation that left the younger ones feeling confused, hurt, and betrayed. My sister, however, was joyous; now she, too, could have the cornrows she had, up till then, been denied because of her race. When she brought home this piece of information, our mother had no choice but to relent and braid Alexandra's hair as best she could, putting in black, red, and orange African beads as my sister requested. It was all to no avail. The braids frayed, and the beads didn't stand out against her chestnut hair; rather, they looked like colored gnats or lice that had infested her scalp. My sister was not entirely satisfied with my mother's effort, but she wanted to show Adoonie nonetheless, so she rushed out to the playground to find her.

"Yo, excuse me, miss," an older girl said and laughed, "someone left some twine on your head."

"Is that some cornrows?" another asked, stopping from her jump-rope counting game. "Looks more like wheat to me."

"Oh, snap," added a third, cracking up.

Alexandra started crying and ran back into the pitted brick building. When Adoonie found her upstairs, she tried to console her. "My mother will do your braids for you if you like." She stroked my sister's head as she spoke softly to her. "Won't that be nice, wouldn't you like that?"

"Forget it," Alexandra said as she unwound the cornrows, which had already started to unbraid themselves as if they, too, didn't like how the experiment had turned out. "I don't want the stupid cornrows. They're stupid." At this comment, Adoonie cried and ran off. From then on Alexandra only wanted long blonde hair, straight as could be, taking comfort in the cultural value of her whiteness.

It didn't take more than one or two messages like this to drive home the meaning of race to my sister. Race was not something mutable, like a freckle or a hairstyle; it defined who looked like whom, who was allowed to be in the group—and who wasn't. But for Alexandra and me, race was turned inside-out. Notwithstanding the Barbie incident, the cornrows, and the images we saw on television, we had no idea that we belonged to the majority group, the privileged one. We merely thought we didn't belong.

That began to change for me when I started at the local public school, across Pitt Street on the other side of the housing complex. By then I had learned that I was white and other people around me weren't, but I had yet to understand what that difference meant. I had yet to learn the privileges that attended whiteness. One month in public school would fix that.

On the first day of classes that fall, the principal called my mother and me into his office. "Mrs. Cone-ly," he said in a heavy Puerto Rican accent, "can I speak with you for a moment?" The school was Public School 4, the Mini School, named for its diminutive size. However, the moniker reflected nothing about the size of the classes. There were only three, each of them overcrowded with about forty students.

"We do not have a class for your son," the principal told my mother, looking down and smiling at me; I remember staring, transfixed, at his snakeskin boots, feeling as if they might slither around the floor of his office if I took my eyes off them. "You see," he continued, "there is the black and Puerto Rican classes." The words *Puerto Rican* stood out from the rest; they seemed to spring naturally from his mouth, whereas the English words dropped out like stillborns. "And then there is the Chinese class . . . ," he trailed off, as if he regretted the Chinese class. "There have been many Chinese that come here now." They were coming from an ever-expanding Chinatown, which had crept into the other side of the school district.

My mother didn't quite follow him. She wondered whether the fact that the principal did not speak English too well meant I would learn Spanish in this school. I remember only his attire, every detail of it. Over his snakeskin boots he wore a beige polyester suit and matching tie. The jacket had many buttons, so that it looked more like a shirt than the upper half of a suit.

"So, which class do you prefer?" he asked, fingering one of the buttons.

It now dawned on my mother that school desegregation did not necessarily mean classroom desegregation. She still had not answered the principal, who now took it upon himself to explain further. "You see," he added, "there is no white class." He now reclined, crossed his arms, and smiled, content that he had finally gotten his point across.

"I suppose we'll take the black class," she said, trying to guess which one my father would have chosen. In this instance, the choices our race gave us were made quite explicit—by a government institution, no less.

I found myself in a crowded classroom with paint peeling from the walls and plaster falling from the ceiling. The teacher was a black woman with a slender frame but a booming voice. She normally taught fourth or fifth grade and wasn't too happy about being stuck with us first-graders. She paced across the front of the room, intermittently drawing on the blackboard to illustrate what she was saying. Sometimes she would write out big words, forgetting that most of us could not read much more than the alphabet or words like "cat." When not drawing on the board, she compulsively brushed chalk residue off her hands and dress. Nevertheless, as each day wore on the layer of chalk dust covering her got progressively deeper, giving her skin a ghost-like quality, as if she were fading away—along with our attention—during the afternoon hours.

As if to compensate for her weakening skin tone and our waning concentration, she grew stricter by the hour. In the mornings we could get away with whispering or fidgeting in our seats. But by one p.m., any peep or audible rustle meant a whack across the knuckles with a yardstick. For everybody but me, that is.

"Yo, your momma been on welfare so long," my classmate Earl whispered to me, "her face's on food stamps." He gave a low five to the boy seated in front of him, checking first to see that the teacher was still turned toward the blackboard. However, he did not take account of the fact that her hearing improved after the lunch hour.

"Up here right now, Earl," she said. She stood akimbo, fists balled up.

Earl marched up slowly, staring at his sneakers, face down and Afro up, as if it offered protection. It didn't. She took his hands and whacked them three times with the thin edge of the ruler. I felt myself leap off the seat with each whack, as if the ruler were a lever and I were sitting on the other end of it. My spine and head stayed still, but the rest of me moved upward. Then I started to blink, and my cheeks began to twitch. Earl did not flinch or yelp in the least.

He turned around and walked back to his desk with a

stoicism that exceeded his age. When he passed by my seat on the way back to his place, I stared down as he had in the presence of the teacher, unable to look him in the eyes. I remember catching a glimpse of his bloodied knuckles, where his brown skin had parted to reveal the scarlet flesh underneath. I fantasized about being beaten myself, digging the graphite tip of my number-two pencil into my skin. Then I released the pressure, trying to share the sense of relief I imagined Earl felt after his punishment was over. At lunch Earl asked if he could sit next to me. I nodded. Still looking down, I tensed up and twitched, waiting for his blow. It never came. He offered me his Tater Tots. As if he could read my mind, he said, "Aw, she's alright; don't worry about her."

Over the weeks, every kid received this form of corporal punishment, boys and girls alike. Some kids, Earl among them, suffered the ruler's blows so often that their knuckles scabbed and then scarred over into rough keloid skin. I was the only one who escaped the yardstick—and not, I knew even at the time, because I was particularly well behaved. Everyone involved, teacher and students, took it for granted that a black teacher would never cross the racial line to strike a white student. The other kids never resented me for this; on the contrary, they were quite cheerful toward me. I even tried to get into fights in that school, fights I knew I would lose; I wanted to feel the relief of being struck. But Earl, one of the largest kids in the school, took it upon himself to protect me. By the end of my first term there, my mother noticed that I was twitching and blinking compulsively—not just during classroom hours, and not just from the image of the yardstick striking Earl's knuckles. There was something else bothering me. Each day I came home from school trembling and immediately ran to the bathroom to relieve myself. My mother also noticed that my Fruit-of-the-Loom underwear and even some of my Toughskin jeans were urine-stained. She asked me why I didn't go to the bathroom at school.

"If you go to the bathroom," I said, nodding my head to emphasize the seriousness of what I was saying, "they cut off your pee-pee."

"No, they don't cut off your pee-pee," she answered, stroking my head as it jerked repeatedly to the side in one of my many new tics.

"Yes," I nodded exuberantly, quite sure of what I was saying, appearing almost happy at the horrible possibility I was describing. Only when I was deeply engrossed in or completely certain of something did my tics disappear. "If you go to the bathroom, they cut off your pee-pee." I now said it as if I were exasperated at having to explain something so obvious. This was the first time that I used the term *they* to describe the collective other, the same *they* who would commit countless crimes throughout my childhood but a different *they* from those who made the rules for school, set policy on busing, and decided how much rent we paid or how many food stamps we received.

Wanting to get to the bottom of my tics and my reluctance to use the restroom at school, my mother made an appointment with the principal. This time his clothing had changed dramatically. He wore the same gray snakeskin boots, but over them hung not a friendly beige suit but rather a black, urbane one with a matching silk shirt. His tie, which bore a picture of Bugs Bunny, stood in sharp contrast to the gangsterish shirt and jacket. He sat on the edge of his desk, one foot swinging back and forth slowly, as if he were trying to hypnotize my mother. His head motion added to this effect. He nodded rhythmically, as if he were checking out her body. She was wearing her favorite denim jacket with mother-of-pearl buttons, though she could not fasten them across her ample chest. She had sewn a Navajo bead design on the back to force some strange truce between cowboys and Indians in her clothing.

"Does the teacher hit Dalton?" she asked. She had already asked me, and I had said no—but I twitched when I answered the question.

"Oh, no," he answered. "In fact," he added, "Dalton is the only student that is not hit."

Bingo! thought my mother, realizing I had told her the truth. "That must be it," she said to the principal. "That's why he's twitching."

"So you want him to receive physical discipline as well, then?" the principal asked, as if this were the logical conclusion to their conversation. His boots had stopped moving and were now clamped against the side of his desk for balance as he leaned toward her.

"No, no," she said, pushing her glasses back up her nose, as was her habit. She asked whether something could be done to prevent the other kids from being struck.

"No, Mrs. Cone-ly," he explained in a tone that was simultaneously sympathetic and exasperated. He explained that the other parents had requested that their children be physically disciplined. "We knew that white parents spoil their kids," he said, "so she doesn't strike Dalton."

The Puerto Rican class had a Puerto Rican teacher who also hit the students, so the solution that the principal and my mother worked out was to switch me to the Chinese class. The teacher there did not use corporal punishment. Though growing rapidly, the local Asian population was still comparatively small, so the class had the added benefit of having fewer students than the others. I transferred in during the first week of the spring semester. Half the lessons were taught in English, the other half in Chinese. I liked the friendly dynamics of the class and felt challenged by my language handicap. My linguistic disadvantage compensated for the fact that by some error, I had been switched from my first-grade class into kindergarten.

"When I call out your name, stand up," the teacher said during roll call on my first day. "If you have an American name, tomorrow I will tell you your name in Chinese. If you have a Chinese name, tomorrow I will tell you your name in English." I was excited by the prospect of being renamed and merging into the group, of which I was the only non–ethnically Chinese member. The next morning the instructor came in and started the roll call again. This time she read off two names for everyone.

"John," she said. "Jiang. Jaili, Julie." Then she got to me. "Dalton," she said. "Dalton," she repeated.

I was crushed. She announced that she could not find a translation for my name. Of course, at the time I didn't know that none of these name pairs were actual translations, that there was no straightforward way to convert names from a tonal, character-based language to English. Nonetheless, to make me feel better she said my name once again in the second tone, so that it went up in pitch in the latter syllable. She made the entire class repeat it in her Cantonese accent. They did. Instead of feeling better, though, I felt singled out by this attention.

To make matters worse, the next day we went through our birthdays. I found out that everyone else had been born in the year of the dog, 1970, while I—the ostensible first-grader among them—was born in the year of the rooster, 1969. The kids chuckled to themselves, but their laughter did not wound me the way the snaps of some of the black kids had. This, I would later realize, captured the essential difference between race and ethnicity. It would have seemed absurd if the black teacher had tried to integrate me into that class. Racial groupings were about domination and struggles for power; what's more, race barriers were taken as both natural and insurmountable.

But in the Chinese class, eventually I began to feel I was part of the student community. My Chinese language skills improved, and my black hair grew longer and straighter—as if I were unconsciously trying to assimilate—so that by the end of the first month my mother confessed she could not pick me out instantly when she came to walk me home from school.

While life was for the most part more comfortable for me in the Chinese class, I made no real friends there, no one that I saw after school. Most of the kids lived west of the school, on the other side of the district, and were picked up promptly at three o'clock by their grandparents, who generally spoke no English and shepherded them home by their wrists. I must have already started to segregate myself culturally, since it never even crossed my mind to invite any of the kids home with me after school. At the same time, I had lost touch with most of my friends from the black class, who lived scattered among the housing projects and tenements of my neighborhood.

After I switched classes my tics gradually disappeared, and I no longer held my urine all day. My mother asked me if I was, in fact, going to the bathroom at school. "Yes," I responded. "Now they no cut off your pee-pee." My diction had taken on a Chinese rhythm. She laughed, relieved that I had resolved my fears. But soon afterward she read a very disturbing story in the *Daily News*. "Castrator Caught," the headline read. The story went on to explain how several students had lost their genitals in the P.S. 4 bathroom. An angry crowd had finally apprehended this child molester and beat him to death on Delancey Street. I had been right all along.

My parents decided that enough was enough. When the semester ended I was once again yanked from my class, this time bound for another school altogether. That didn't work out either. But then my mother learned from a friend that the Board of Education did not require much in the way of proof of one's address to verify a child's school district. She could tell them she lived in the Empire State Building and, as long as she could get mail there and respond to immunization notices, lice alerts, and other school correspondence, no one would ever be the wiser. It was even the case, she learned, that after October 1 she could switch my address back to the projects and, since the school year would already be under way, the Board of Education could not force me to return to my local school. What's more, once October rolled around, my adopted school was legally required—thanks to the liberal New York State courts—to send a bus to pick me up and take me home.

A small group of enterprising parents from the neighborhood had enough crosstown contacts to take advantage of these loopholes. They spent the first month of each academic year carting their kids across town on the subway or the M14 bus to schools in well-endowed districts; once the October 1 deadline came, a yellow school bus would swoop into the projects, rounding up the fortunate kids. Each year the dance would begin anew. The schools that were inundated with us "ghetto" kids didn't mind the arrangement, since we took funds with us wherever we went. Title I of the Elementary and Secondary Education Act of 1965, one of the cornerstones of Lyndon Johnson's Great Society, provided federal funds for students from economically distressed areas, be they the dirt farms of eastern Kentucky or the dirt-colored buildings of the Lower East Side. Title I kids, as we were called, benefited by getting better educations, while the schools themselves won out financially. The losers in the arrangement were the local schools, which lost not only funding but also the students whose parents enjoyed the most "social capital," that is, connections.

The *they* who made up these policies were, on the surface, quite different in character from the *they* who stole car radios or cut off the peckers of my classmates at the Mini School. The Board of Education, the state welfare agency, and all the other *they*s who set the rules of our lives seemed obsessed with laws and regulations. They wrote them, implemented them, followed them, and in some cases were actually composed of them and nothing more. Beneath the surface, however, these state behemoths were no different in nature from the spirits who stole; they were just as arbitrary, random, and mysterious. One rule said you had to go to school where you lived; another said that where you "lived" was your choice. One law gave extra money to underfunded school districts; another took it away and gave it to better-off districts. It seemed possible to get whatever you wanted as long as you knew the magic words and when to say them. It was through such a spell that I was propelled off the life trajectory shared by the other neighborhood kids and catapulted into New York City's middle and upper classes. My life chances had just taken a turn for the better, but my sense of the order of things—that is, the pecking order of race and class—was about to be stood on its head.

By the time I left the Mini School I had learned what the concept of race meant. I now knew that, based on the color of my skin, I would be treated a certain way, whether that entailed not getting rapped across the knuckles, not having a name like everyone else, or not having the same kind of hair as my best friend. Some kids got unique treatment for being taller or heavier than everyone else, but being whiter than everyone else was a different matter altogether. Teachers usually did a good job of ignoring the fact that one kid was shorter than another or another was fatter, but it was they, not the other students, who made my skin color an issue. The kids had only picked up on the adult cues and then reinterpreted them. Moreover, height, weight, and other physical characteristics were relative states. But being white was constructed as a matter of kind, not degree. Either you were black, or you weren't. Some of the kids in my original first-grade class were *blancitos*—lighter-skinned Puerto Ricans—but that didn't mean that they got rapped on the knuckles any softer than the darker-skinned kids. Once you weren't a *blanco*, it didn't matter what your skin color was in P.S. 4.

At my new school, the name of the game was class. That brought a whole new set of rules. And it would take me a while to learn them.

The steel door to our apartment was my security blanket. Behind it I was safe from the school castrator. I was safe from muggers. I was safe from other kids. My fear of assault was as constant as the bellowing of my lungs; I was only occasionally aware of it, only when it had ceased to be breathing and turned into panting.

My mother had instructed my sister and me over and over again about what to do in certain emergency situations. This preparing for the worst made me more afraid on a day-to-day basis, but that was part of her plan. She had programmed us with a series of computer-like algorithms. "Do whatever someone with a gun says to do," was one of her instructions, "unless they tell you to get into a car. Never get into a car with anyone. Run or scream." Another stricture: "Always lock the door. Never open it until you have a) asked who it is, b) looked through the peephole, c) recognized who it is, or d) seen that it's the police."

Not until I encountered people who grew up with unlocked screen doors did I realize that not everyone lived most of their waking hours behind a steel barricade. Not until I met people who lived in one- or two-story homes did I realize that most kids don't worry about beer bottles raining down on their heads from the balconies above, as I did on Friday and Saturday nights. Taking out the garbage, I always opened the door to the incinerator room with trepidation, terrified that someone would pounce on me. When I picked up the laundry from the washing machines in the basement, there was occasionally a character lurking in the shadows—and not merely one from a child's imagination. In these instances I would scurry up the stairs to the lobby and wait for the elevator there rather than sit in the basement with the potential predator. Often I told my mother about these shadowy figures, and she would summon the authorities to go down and inspect the scene; sometimes arrests were made. If an elevator stopped and I didn't like the look of the person inside I wouldn't get on, feigning that it was going in the wrong direction. But the place I feared most of all was the stairwell—and with good reason, for more than once someone was raped or mugged in there.

Whenever all the elevators were broken, I would have to walk all twenty-one flights of that windowless cement hole. On some floors the lights were out, and I would traverse a story or two in complete blackness. Other times I would force myself to confront my fear, choosing the stairwell instead of the elevator for a flight or two. The gray, graffitied fire route wove itself into my nightmares. I dreamed I was trapped in it; I was fleeing something, my legs tiring with each passing moment, and there were no exits.

By early in my childhood I had cultivated a keen sense of caution probably not unlike that developed by soldiers in the bush. Walking down the street, I had an awareness of what was going on around me that someone who grew up in the suburbs would have had great difficulty acquiring. However, several events kept my illusions of my own streetwiseness and security in check. The first came when a family was robbed and killed a few blocks from us. The assailants gained entry to the victims' house by dressing up as policemen. That changed my mother's door-opening rule; I was now to keep the police waiting until I had called the station to confirm that they had been sent over.

The second event happened to us and completely shattered my sense of our apartment as a fortress. One weekend we went to visit my grandparents and left the kitchen window open. On the twenty-first floor this should not have been a problem, the biggest risk being that rain might come through the window. However, a cat burglar tied the fire hose to the railing around the perimeter of the roof and swung into our apartment. Once inside, he ignored the sticker my mother had posted that read BEWARE, WE PARTICIPATE IN OPERATION IDEN-TIFICATION, NYPD and waltzed out the front door loaded down with our belongings, which my mother had etched with a se-cret code that the police could track in the case of an event such as this one. The burglar must have made several trips, be-cause he took our television, our radio, the silverware that my parents had gotten as a wedding present, our plates and glasses, even a couple of pieces of furniture. When we got back from Pennsylvania, we saw the door ajar. My father made the rest of us wait in the hallway while he tiptoed into the apartment. He surveyed the damage, noticed the open kitchen window, slammed it shut, and locked it. My stairwell nightmares were soon replaced by bad dreams about a robber floating twenty-one stories above ground, hovering outside our window. In my dreams he looked like José, the overdose victim portrayed on the Avenue D mural. He had the same goatee and devilish smile.

Not much later the burglar struck again. We returned from a trip to find the door once again ajar, this time with a trail of blood leading over to the window, which we had closed and locked. That, however, had not deterred this daredevil. He used the same tactic as the first time, but on this occasion crashed through the window glass like the star of an action film. There wasn't much left to steal, so he took the few bottles of wine my father kept. We went to a friend's home for a few nights while my father slept in the apartment, hoping to catch the robber and bean him with his Ted Williams baseball bat, but the crook never returned.

My parents decided that the only thing we could do was to install gates in the windows. Unfortunately, they ran in the thousands of dollars, money that we didn't have. The cheapest alternatives, which cost several hundred dollars—most of our savings—were black steel bars that were bolted into the window frame and could not be removed except by taking apart the entire window jamb. From then on we lived in a prison-like apartment unit, wriggling our hands through the bars whenever we wanted to open or shut the window.

Thanks to their days on Seventh Street, when their television was chained to the radiator, my parents were familiar with being robbed. But this was the first time it had happened to me. Crime and violence were not uncommon in our area, but they always seemed to happen elsewhere and, I believed, could be avoided, like the beer bottles falling from the sky. Even the castrations at school didn't feel like a personal threat; I merely had to avoid the bathroom to avoid danger. But the prospect of someone crashing through our twenty-first-floor window was frightening on another level. It meant I was not even safe in my own bed, not even behind our locked double-steel front door. In short, there was nothing I could do to escape risk. Only in retrospect did I realize that break-ins were not a common occurrence for most families in America and that having bars on the windows was not normal.

But in our case it was necessary. After we installed the bars, my nightmares finally waned. I felt protected from the outside world. I also felt safer playing indoors; prior to the window guards, I had always been nervous whenever my friends and I played catch or tackle football or tag in the house. I feared one of us would hurl ourselves through the window or, more realistically, toss a ball or toy through the glass and kill a pedestrian all those stories below.

Often I hung on those black bars, my hands gripping them so tightly that the cartilage of my knuckles shone white through my skin, as I stared down at the other project kids playing whiffle ball or ring-a-levio or manhunt. Manhunt was my favorite project game, and I would cross the barrier of the bars anytime to play. While kids could play caps or ring-a-levio throughout the entire year, manhunt was reserved for the hottest months. The game was simple. One person was selected as the hunted. He got a fifteen-minute head start and could hide anywhere in the housing complex. Soon afterward, the several dozen or so boys would go out in search of the hunted. The prey could not go into apartments but had to stay in the public spaces such as hallways, alleys, and rooftops. If no one found him the game could last all day.

After a year or two of playing manhunt I got quite skilled at it. I enjoyed being hunted, outwitting kids several years older than myself. In fact, I was only ever caught once, and that was the last day I played. I was supposed to be cleaning up my room. Instead I sneaked out of the apartment around the time I knew manhunt would be commencing. I immediately volunteered for the role of the hunted, and when the game started I took off to the project basements, which were linked into one huge, dimly lit cavern. My strategy for that day was simple: I hid in a dark corner of one of the less well-known rooms in the basement, shimmying up the pipes and perching overhead, careful not to touch the steam conduits that would have scalded me. Several times I heard approaching footsteps and whispers and held my breath, but for the most part this was a quite relaxing, even boring, tactic. It lacked the heart-pounding adrenaline rush that came with an on-the-move strategy, where one always stayed just a step ahead of the posse. I was so well hidden that at one point that day I even took a nap, checking my watch every so often as I waited for the five o'clock hour to approach, signaling the end of the game and victory for me.

My mother spoiled my plans, however. Furious that I had disobeyed her by sneaking out, she stormed into the central area of the project, grabbed the first kid she saw and demanded to know where I was.

"I dunno," responded Angel, who despite his name and his timid answer was one of the tougher kids around. "We're looking for where he's at, too." She listened as he recounted the rules of the game to her. Then he ran off and reported his encounter to some of the other kids. A group of them collected around my mother, following her like a brood as she stalked me—and trampled on the entire premise of the game. She marched into the central security office and asked if she could sit in front of the video monitors. Aided by her maternal instincts, she watched as the images flickered across the screens, one after another. Eventually she recognized my figure and asked the guard to freeze on that shot. The guard explained to my mother exactly where I had installed myself and how to get there, and then she descended into the basement to retrieve me, trailed by the manhunters, who were eager to watch me get a whipping.

I wish she had hit me. I heard the sound of a whole bunch of footsteps coming toward me. "Oh snap," I remember hearing one of the kids say. "Now he's going to get it." Somehow I knew instantly that this was no mere pack of kids that had come to win the game or even to beat me senseless. I could feel my mother's presence. I turned to see who was approaching and made immediate eye contact with her.

"This instant," she said, and nothing more.

The kids surrounding her were all shaking their hands rapidly, our signal for someone getting busted. "Ooooh," they said as they made this gesture, which looked as if they were trying to signal the spiciness of something they had just bitten into.

I hung down from one of the pipes and dropped to the ground. My mother immediately grabbed me by the ear and dragged me alongside her. Instead of weaving our way to our own building in the underground passageways, she took the first stairs she saw out of the basement and into the bright June light. Kids followed, taunting me. "You lost, you lost to your momma!" they yelled as she dragged me through the playgrounds so that everyone could see. We passed the coach of my little league baseball team, Las Piratas, who was sitting on the bench, smoking his menthol cigarettes. Right then and there she gave me my punishment: she wrapped her arms around me and gave me a big kiss, overemphasizing the smacking sound of her pucker. I ran home and cleaned up my room. The pleasure of manhunt had been forever spoiled.

In retrospect, manhunt was not a strange game for us to be playing. Unlike baseball or football, it taught us important skills for life in the "ghetto." It trained the hunted to evade both criminals and the police, who in that neighborhood were deemed equivalent. And it socialized the hunters to adopt a posse mentality, one that would become institutionalized among those who joined the local gang, the Junior Outlaws. It may have been through this sense of group unity that my peers achieved the sense of security that forever eluded me.

This is not to say that I didn't try to integrate and hold my own in the group. I studied karate with the express purpose of becoming tough enough to feel secure. My father and I took lessons from a black Muslim *sensei* named Rahim, formerly Robert. He had worked in the Brooklyn shipyards when there still was such a thing, scraping and painting the sides of huge vessels. He spent some time in jail and smoked marijuana on a daily basis. Robert became Rahim after taking up martial arts, studying with a Muslim *sensei* who inspired a life change in his pupil. Rahim quit his job, stopped smoking pot, and devoted his life to the Koran, supporting himself in a haphazard, catch-as-catch-can manner.

We were Rahim's only white pupils, and I think he might have had reservations about sharing his skills with us but needed whatever work he could get. I encountered some cultural confusion during our training; each time he bent down to pray in the direction of Mecca I thought he was doing something karate-related, perhaps a stretch of some sort. Following his lead, I got in the habit of laying out a towel before each session, kneeling and bending until my forehead touched the ground, and mumbling as if I were reciting some of the Koran. Neither Rahim nor my father ever discouraged the practice. It came in handy when Rahim took us to a tournament in a huge mosque and cultural center in Brooklyn. I was overwhelmed from the moment I arrived; I had never seen a ceiling so high. The strange calligraphy that lined each entranceway and the low-relief designs that crawled up the walls and columns like vines seemed to grow and breathe in some mystical way. As Rahim escorted us into the mat-covered arena, some people stared at us through narrowed eyes as they noticed our whiteness. Everyone else was black; there were not even any Puerto Ricans at this event.

Then the call to prayer came over the loudspeaker, and the milling around ceased instantly; everyone fell into orderly lines. This transformation impressed on me the power of Islam—that a chaotic, seemingly menacing group of people could suddenly organize themselves into perfect rows, like schoolchildren more disciplined than any I had ever seen. Even my anti-religious father fell into line, and we all bowed to Mecca. The familiarity of this rite felt comforting, and once it had taken place the aura of tension dissipated, replaced by a sense of spirited competition. I won in the first round but lost in the second of the single-elimination tournament, but that was good enough. I had earned my yellow belt.

Though I had moved up a rank in the karate hierarchy, my association with Rahim did not achieve the intended purpose of making me feel safer and more secure in the neighborhood, and for a simple reason: within a year Rahim was shot and killed. Evidently, even a black belt did little against a gun; in fact, it may have been a detriment. By the account of his widow, Rahim had resisted a mugging, using his fighting ability to fend off his attackers until one of them pulled out a pistol and shot him. Somehow I imagined him dressed up in his karate *gi*, being picked on because of his garb the way I was when I wore my outfit down in the playground. Others who knew him shook their heads and whispered to my father that he had been shot twice in the head at point-blank range. For once I listened quietly, discovering that I could learn more by not asking anything than by opening my mouth. The implication was that this had been no random robbery but that Rahim had been assassinated for a reason: drugs.

This was the first time violence had entered our lives in a serious, personal way. I tried to envision Rahim lying motionless, dead, but I could keep him still in my mind only for as long as I imagined he could hold his breath; after about a minute he would spring up, gasping for air. I suppose they held a memorial service for him in the same mosque where my father and I had fought for our new belt colors, but we were never invited; not having seen his corpse, I still could not quite clothe Rahim in death. Eventually, I asked my father which story about the killing he believed. He raised his eyebrows at me, apparently shocked that I had heard the adult whispers going back and forth above my head. "I don't know," he said. "There are some things that we will never know." He rubbed the scar tissue of his face and punched the plastic keys of his calculator a little harder than normal. My father always said more with his silences, his pauses, and the movement of his fingers to his face than he did with his words. He communicated the mystery and uncertainty of life in a way that my mother never could.

I wanted to think that Rahim had been the victim of random fate, of chaotic violence; however, this explanation seemed as forced and restless as my image of his corpse itself. Somehow I had already developed a keen sense that crime and violence in our neighborhood were not random at all but followed certain patterns. The great, dangerous *they* who committed crimes were neither unthinking nor uncalculating. Why, for instance, didn't the cat burglar break into Kenny's apartment down the hall instead of ours? Was it because we were white?

This innate sense that a larger order undergirded all the murders and stabbings and break-ins made them all the more eerie, as if they followed the scripted steps of a ballroom waltz. I wanted to believe Rahim's widow's version of events, but I couldn't. At the same time, it didn't sit right with me that his devotion to the Koran had been a sham, a lie to himself and to us. It sickened me to realize that the most disciplined, upstanding man I knew might have been involved in something illicit. It was as if the ordered rows of worshippers at the mosque had dissolved back into a noisy throng—that everything, not just Rahim, contained within it its opposite. It didn't help that my father wouldn't tell me definitively what had happened or that no one was ever prosecuted or even arrested for the crime. This lack of resolution gave me my first unsettling taste of powerlessness in the face of uncertainty. Rahim's death preyed on my sense of morality like a dark lesion. Before it, there were lies and there was truth, but I always knew which was which and figured others did as well. But in this case no one would ever know what really happened; it was merely a matter of what each individual chose to believe. There were two truths, and there were none.

My new school, P.S. 41, was only a couple miles from where Rahim was murdered, but it might as well have been in Europe. It stood in Greenwich Village, an upscale neighborhood but one with fewer luxuries than other, wealthier areas of Manhattan. Doormen weren't as ubiquitous there as in other white areas of the island, and the buildings—mostly small brownstones—did not look much different from many of the tenements in my neighborhood. They were just in better condition. It was as if the flower box movement had succeeded on this side of town. Apartments the same size as those burned-out slums on Avenue D sold for hundreds of thousands of dollars apiece in the Village.

The kids there were predominantly white and, by New York standards, middle class—but rich by the norms of the rest of America. We had appropriated the address of one of my parents' artist friends to get me enrolled in P.S. 41, also known as the Greenwich Village School. However, by the time my address change had been recorded and duly processed by the huge educational bureaucracy of New York City, the school year had already started, so I was the new kid once again. To make matters worse, I had been inexplicably jumped a grade, up to third, so now I was younger than everyone else. I stumbled through the morning in a numb haze. Everyone was white and dressed differently from what I was used to. The kids at the Mini School always wore well-pressed clothes; even their variously hued denim pants had ironed creases down the front. I was always the sloppiest kid at P.S. 4; but at P.S. 41, many competed with me for that title. While I had always been ashamed of my appearance at the Mini School, the wrinkle-clad kids here exuded a confidence that seemed to belie their attire. Also, both the students and the teachers talked differently—like the characters on television except more lazily, without moving their mouths much. The kids spoke softly, as if telling secrets to each other; at least, that's how it felt to me on the first day. The teachers also spoke softly; there was no yelling on the part of adults here.

At lunch I spotted the two kids who had answered the most questions during the morning session. In my first two years of schooling, I had been socialized into thinking that kids who showed off how much they knew were outcasts, nerds. At P.S. 4 I always avoided answering the teacher's questions in class. Moreover, I was terrified that the other kids might make some causal connection between my performance and my being spared the rod; they might conclude that I was "on the teacher's side." Since these two kids had violated that norm, I felt they would be more approachable, perhaps even glad to have a new friend. I approached them with my tray of milk, potato puffs, sloppy joe, and pallid succotash—my standard lunchroom fare for many years. They were talking about the meaning of a big word and didn't notice me. I stood above them for a few long moments, turning pink with embarrassment, then finally said: "Can I sit here?"

"I don't know," said one, a blond, tall kid. "Can he sit here?"

"I don't know," said the other one, who was shorter, thicker, and darker, a squashed, brunette version of the blond kid. "Do you know what antidisestablishmentarianism is?" he asked me.

Not even the meanest snap about how poor my momma was had a fraction of the ego-slamming effect this question had. It felt as if a door had been shut in my face. My first instinct was to run and cry. My second was to yell at these two, call them motherfuckers or something else they would have been called back in my neighborhood. My third impulse was to answer their question. I could, in fact, answer it, since they had just been defining the word twenty seconds earlier when they were oblivious to my presence.

"An-ti-dis-es-tab-lish-men-tar-i-an-ism," I said carefully, as if I were in a spelling bee, "means going against one's own beliefs." I changed their wording slightly in order to disguise the fact that I was merely cribbing from their own definition. I prayed that they wouldn't ask me to elaborate or to use the word in a sentence. I blinked—a vestigial twitch from my first-grade days—and looked down at them. Both of their mouths were agape. The blond-headed one slid over to make room and silently beckoned me to join them.

They included me in their conversation, which ranged in

subject from making crystal radios to that year's presidential election. I knew nothing about crystal radios and not much about the election either. Nevertheless, I hung in there, hiding my ignorance by picking up conversational cues, all the while trying to decipher the internal logic of the discussion so that I could participate as well. I had learned this technique through countless discussions of *Happy Days* back at my old school. Though I tried my hardest, I couldn't stay awake until 8 p.m. each Tuesday night, when that show, the favorite of all the kids at the Mini School, aired. So each Wednesday, I would sit quietly during the first ten minutes of recess and work out the previous night's plot while listening to the others argue about the show—which scene was funniest, which character's antics were most entertaining, and so on. Before long I would jump in on one side of the debate or another. It didn't matter which one, as long as I was part of the argument, making reference to past shows—which I also hadn't seen—to bolster my position. Those morning rituals were some of the few occasions on which I felt part of the group; arguing always meant a loss of self-consciousness on my part.

I fell back on those skills as Michael, the blond kid, argued for Jimmy Carter, and Ozan, the dark-haired Turkish kid, stumped for Gerald Ford. I listened, having only a vague notion of who these figures were. I knew they were important people, but my knowledge about anything political was limited. Such matters did not often get debated in our house. Later that day, during afternoon recess, I capitalized on the

knowledge I had gained at lunch and spoke at a schoolyard political rally that Michael and Ozan had organized.

Greenwich Village was, and still is, one of the most liberal
districts in the entire United States. All of the kids except
Ozan preferred Carter, no doubt mimicking their parents;
therefore I, too, jumped on the Democratic side. After
Michael spoke out in favor of Carter, I volunteered to second
him. I told the group how Carter would fix a number of things
ranging from inflation to Watergate, none of which I had even
heard of until lunchtime that day. The rush was intense: Not
only was I a part of the group, the group was me. During those
two minutes, I had shed the role of new kid.

Then Ozan spoke, and he was even more eloquent, as well-
spoken as a third grader could be. Whether because of his
rhetorical brilliance or because the other kids threw their support to whomever was the last person to speak, by the end of
his soliloquy Ford was clearly winning the P.S. 41 schoolyard.
Then something else happened that neither Ozan nor I could
have predicted. One of the girls in our class, whose father, she
informed us, was somehow connected to Jimmy Carter, offered free Dunkin' Donuts to anyone who voted for the Dem-
ocrat. She held open a box, and a stampede of kids left Ozan's
symbolic soapbox to crowd around the doughnut box. I was
among them.

Ozan knew he had lost in the face of free doughnuts, but he
still kept yelling to the crowd. "You can't say 'I vote for
Carter,' " he shouted. "You can't vote for Carter!" He was

barely audible over the din of "me toos" that surrounded the doughnut girl. "The Twenty-sixth Amendment of the U.S. Constitution lowered the voting age to eighteen, but we can't vote for anyone; we can only root. You can't vote; you can only root," he repeated desperately, as if so much hung on the distinction. He looked as though he might cry. I felt an inkling of sympathy, but it did not override my joy at being on the right side, with the in-group.

The girl heard him and laughed, "Free Dunkin' Donuts to anyone who 'roots' for Carter." The kids shrieked with delight. When everyone had gotten one and there were still a couple left, she stopped and shooed away the kids who were begging for seconds. "Ozan," she called over to him. "I'll give you one, too. I'll even give you two, if you just say that you like Carter." She paused. "You don't even have to vote or root for him; just say you like him." Ozan looked down at the pieces of deep-fried dough, glistening with glaze. I could see the longing in his dark eyes. Everyone in the schoolyard was quiet, waiting to see if he would sacrifice political principle for fast food.

"No," he said at last. "I am for Ford because he is better; keep your Dunkin' Donuts." Within a few seconds the last couple had been accounted for, and the empty box blew across the schoolyard. We were called back into class. When I went home later that day, I kept thinking about Ozan's last stand. I had never seen such willpower in a third grader—or anyone else for that matter, young or old, rich or poor.

This was a lesson not only about class but also about the status of immigrants. Back in my neighborhood, it didn't seem to make much difference whether someone's family had been in New York for a while or had just arrived from Puerto Rico or the Dominican Republic. The local culture seemed to be in constant dialogue with those Caribbean islands; we took Hispanic kids on their own terms, even absorbed some of their language and customs. Ozan, by contrast, seemed to carry the mark of foreignness with him through the halls of P.S. 41. It wasn't about race, for he appeared as white as anyone else. It might have been about ethnicity, since his name certainly set him off from the rest of us. But the major division between Ozan and everyone else was of his own making: his political opinions, almost as a rule, diverged from those of the rest of class. I found myself swayed by his intelligence and eloquent arguments on many occasions, but I resisted falling into his camp since it would have meant ostracizing myself. Ozan seemed able to handle that, but it was the last thing I wanted in a class full of people who were white like me, only more so.

Only more so—this was the fact that had dislodged my identity that first dazed day at P.S. 41. Suddenly, being white was no longer the marker that set me off from everybody else, that defined who I was. Being a honky may have made me twitch back at the Mini School, but it also gave me a certain freedom to act however I wanted, since people's reactions never reflected anything about me in particular but could always be brushed off as a racial thing. For instance, despite their tradition of snapping on each other, most of the kids didn't make a big deal of my tics; maybe they thought that was how most white people behaved. Only after this special status was gone did I appreciate its benefits. It was like being a U.S. citizen overseas—feeling intensely American, almost like a diplomat, and yet more liberated than one would in the United States. Now, at P.S. 41, I was just myself, with no racial line to protect me and no people to represent.

When I got home after that first day in the Village, I rushed upstairs, avoiding any of the kids from my old school who might be hanging out on the benches or on the jungle gym. I felt ashamed of the pleasure I had experienced that day at school. P.S. 41 seemed like a far-off land, a place of sophistication and luxury. The classes were relatively small, and I didn't have to be wary of showing my knowledge. I had lots of catching up to do in the category of general learning. There were so many things they knew about, not just crystal radios and politics but also physics and astronomy. And they knew lots of words, words almost as big as *antidisestablishmentarianism*. I had suddenly been awakened to how many things I didn't know. Every day I wrote down the list of words I had heard or saw whose meaning I didn't know. Then each night I would ask my parents what they meant. I made a list of the state capitals, taped it up on my wall, and memorized each one. Then I moved on to the countries of the world and their capitals, memorizing those too and pasting them up on the wall. I made lists of everything. One night after Michael taught me what square roots were, I stayed up past midnight, forgetting all about *Happy Days*, and sat in my room with one of my father's calculators, making a list of the square root of every number from one to a hundred. The next week I learned what prime numbers were and made a list of those. My walls were getting full and my brain saturated. I stayed up each night trying to detect mathematical patterns that had been previously unnoticed in the string of prime numbers.

Then, one afternoon at Michael's house, his father, who was a professor of psychology at NYU, asked me how long it would take me to get home if every five minutes I walked half the remaining distance. I was baffled and amazed to realize that when I had gone halfway home I'd be somewhere in the Russian section of Second Avenue, and that when I had gone halfway again I would be standing outside the headquarters of the New York City Hell's Angels, until eventually I'd be stuck somewhere right at the entrance to my building, practically unable to move, even more immobile than the elderly residents who hobbled up to the glass-and-steel door and waited for someone to open it for them. After Zeno's paradox, Michael's dad went on to explain some of the properties of zero to me, specifically that any number divided by zero was infinity. This set me off on another obsession. I spent the next few days drawing up a whole set of rules for dividing, multiplying, and combining infinity and zero.

I spent so much time on my geography and math fixations that I did almost no schoolwork. The only problems that interested me were ones that weren't already solved. I had not yet learned that eight times nine was seventy-two, but I didn't care, because everybody already knew that. The time I was supposed to be memorizing multiplication tables I spent trying to break the four-color map rule. I had decided there was no point in doing anything that was not original, that wasn't big, really big. My grades were mediocre, and my teacher consistently claimed on my report card that I was not "performing up to potential." But I was not after her accolades; I sought approval from Michael and his father.

The dynamics between Michael and me reflected a type of status hierarchy that simply did not exist at my old school in either the black or Chinese class. At first I didn't understand why Michael was popular, since he was nerdier than most of the other students. But I was beginning to realize that each student possessed a sense of self-worth that translated into a certain position on the social ladder. Only much later did I realize that school dynamics and one's sense of self-worth could not be isolated from family background. It was no coincidence, I would learn, that the most popular kids tended to be those whose parents were the richest or most powerful or held the most prestigious jobs. In my old school there had been no such hierarchy of which I was aware—probably because no one's parents were rich, powerful, or prestigious in any sense of the word. There, each kid invented his own place in the social network. The pecking order was, as best I could tell, determined primarily by brute force, by who could beat up whom. Other qualities mattered too, like athletic prowess, ability to snap, and overall sense of humor.

Nobody at P.S. 4 possessed the class confidence that oozed out of some of the kids at the Greenwich Village School. Only by spending time with some of them after class, in their homes, did I make a connection between the relative opulence of their residences, the profession, style, and grace of their parents, and how they behaved and were treated by the other kids at school. I was learning the language of class, the same dialect that my father once spoke in Connecticut but had long ago given up, like the mother tongue of an immigrant who wishes to shed his past.

I was now a part-time, after-school honky, returning to the projects on the school bus each afternoon while most of my classmates at P.S. 41 sauntered home through safe Greenwich Village streets lined with brownstones, wrought-iron fences, and functioning tree wells devoid of heroin needles or other garbage. Michael and Ozan could decide on the spur of the moment to go to the science fiction bookstore to flip through paperbacks or try out the newest board game. When they went across the street to get a slice at Ray's Pizza after school, I felt the power of class in a different way than I had the first time I met them. This time there was no way I could be sneaky, picking up contextual cues to insinuate myself into their plans. There was no magic word like *antidisestablishmentarianism* that would gain me entry. The fact was that I had no money for pizza—and even if I had, I had no choice but to board the yellow school bus that carted me home to the projects, from which I had begun to feel estranged.

The bus rides served as my transitional period each day, the time during which I took off one face and put on another. The class consciousness I'd begun to acquire at P.S. 41 made me feel extremely grateful for the advantages I had over my neighbors back at home. I had never been aware of my privilege vis-à-vis Earl and the other kids while I went to school with them. It was only when I suffered on the losing side of class distinctions across town that I began to reevaluate my situation within my neighborhood. It was only then that I felt better than those around me. It was a strange combination: I felt humbly thankful for the opportunities I was enjoying at P.S. 41 yet simultaneously was developing a sense of superiority over my old neighbors. This quiet feeling of snobbery was a way of displacing my sense of class inadequacy onto people who I now saw as even lower down on the ladder than me. The process had begun my very first day at P.S. 41. Within a year it had bloomed into full-scale class confusion.

"Yo, your momma's like railroad tracks," one of the other commuter kids yelled at me on the bus ride home from school one particular afternoon during fourth grade. "Everyone lays her down."

I wasn't paying much attention and gave no response. I was too busy thinking about Michael and Ozan eating at Ray's Pizza, discussing the Middle East or some other world hot spot. Without even listening, I could predict the litany of snaps, if not their actual order. There were only a few kids who actually composed new ones off the tops of their heads. Everyone else just recirculated jokes that had been in existence for as long as we could remember.

"Your momma's like a refrigerator," the same person called

out—more to everyone else than to me, though I was still the reference point of the joke. "Everyone sticks their meat in." This time the snap registered more clearly in my head; the kids had broken my daydream. Still, I didn't respond. Now others jumped in: "Your mother's like the M14 bus. Fiddy cent and hop on." None of us knew anything about sex yet, except that it was bad to have it be said that your mother partook of it. It was just another subject for snapping, the same as poverty or ugly sneakers. "Your mother's like a doorknob," a third person added. "Everybody takes their turn."

It was nothing personal against me; I just happened to be the target of the day. It was as if we were all on a roulette wheel, and sometimes my number came up. My role was to duck and parry these snaps, counterpunching when possible, and eventually everyone would break out laughing. But instead of making the requisite tooth-sucking and hissing sounds that implied I thought little of the jokes and dared them to offer something better, I did nothing. Nor did I snap back about their fathers being gay, the roaches in their apartments, or what they ate for dinner. People seemed amazed that I didn't respond. After a while the tone of their voices changed, and their snaps came out less like statements and more like questions, as if they were asking me for approval. They searched me with hopeful eyes, wondering if I would bless their particular snap with a response.

That day I learned the power of silence—that if used appropriately it was more potent than most things that could be said in its place. It was also one of the tools used by the popular kids at P.S. 41 and was itself not unrelated to class. In society overall it may be that those who are in control have a larger voice, the ability to fill up the newspapers and airwaves with their opinions; but on the day-to-day level of the schoolyard it was the less powerful who spoke more, clamoring to be heard by the reserved, better-off kids, who seemed to quietly pass judgment.

I looked forward to each Tuesday, when I didn't have to take the bus home and instead could amble down the Avenue of the Americas with Michael and his friends on our way to a pre-arranged sleepover at his house. We passed the gourmet shops, where salmon and whitefish stared at me out of bulbous eyes and the fresh vegetables tantalized me with colors I had never seen anywhere else. My sense of what was exotic in food was probably the reverse of the other P.S. 41 kids'. It amazed me to glimpse oranges bursting with an *orange* color that I had otherwise only seen in artificially flavored candy. Pineapples at the Jefferson Market looked like those worn on the hats of ladies in the cartoons. Pink grapefruit was really pink. In the Pioneer Supermarket and the bodegas on the Lower East Side, all the citrus fruits—be they lemons, oranges, or tangerines—were the same yellowish color. My mother called the produce selection at Pioneer "used vegetables." By contrast, the broccoli, spinach, and lettuce at Balducci's on Sixth Avenue were such a bright green that they were almost enticing to my third-grade palate.

When our teacher assigned us to go shopping with our parents, write out a list of items by food group, and declare whether we thought they were nutritious, I had a hard time. The little bodegas that dotted most corners in my neighborhood seemed to display fresh offerings, but their papayas, plantains, yuccas, and taro roots were not listed on the nutritional posters that lined our classroom. I went with my father to the Las Palmas Mercado with our month's supply of food stamps to buy some staples for the house. We purchased a twenty-five pound bag of rice, the short-grained kind favored in the Caribbean; that was easy enough to put on the starch list. Then we picked up some raw sugarcane that my father used to sweeten a vinegar barbecue sauce. I had no idea in which group to place this item. During the summer, we kids loved to chew on a piece of it and suck out the sweet juices, but I also knew that the stalk was used in various recipes, so it didn't seem quite like candy. We also bought taro root as a side dish. Not even my father was sure whether this went in the vegetable or starch category.

Even the money we used to purchase our food was different from the currency used in the Village. Ours was printed on cheap paper and looked not unlike that from the board games I played at Michael's house. It had pictures of the Liberty Bell on it instead of the presidents, and my father tore it out sheet by sheet from little booklets, which made it seem as if we were writing a check. There were even bills for fifty cents. Sometimes we got these small bills back as change; only if our change was practically nothing did we receive actual currency. The U.S. greenbacks my P.S. 41 friends carried captured my eye like gold itself. And the corn, peas, and bright orange carrots I ate at their houses seemed like the cuisine of another country, the America that I knew only from television. I may not have learned the essential food groups from my homework assignment, but I did learn that not even food is immune to the social dynamics of race and class.

At Michael's house I got to—or, rather, had to—try new foods that didn't fit the two categories I was familiar with: Caribbean cuisine and standard American fare. One Tuesday evening, for instance, I had couscous. I was more fascinated with the fact that the name repeated itself than I was with the small, granular pasta itself. I fixated on the name, convinced that any echoed word must be some sort of linguistic oddity. I listened, enraptured, while Mrs. Holt explained that couscous came from North Africa. Later that evening I snuck off to look up the dish in their encyclopedia.

Everything in the Holts' house smelled of instruction. All our activities there had to be educational. Instead of allowing us to play a board game, Michael's mother had us invent one. Instead of being given a radio to listen to, we were given one to take apart and study. And when we wanted to know what something meant, we were sent to the bookshelves to find the appropriate reference book. My father had built bookshelves that lined one wall in our apartment; in fact, other kids in the building marveled at how many books we had, though the number was one-third the Holts' collection. My parents' books could easily be divided into their respective camps. My mother had practically nothing but contemporary fiction. Many of her editions had been bought at library fire sales and still had the plastic covering on them, along with a stamp indicating that they once had been the property of the Hamilton Fish Branch. Others were publishers' remainders with the covers torn off and "99 cents" written in marker on the front page, now the de facto cover. My mother got to read contemporary work when it had just left the realm of contemporary, with about the same time lag that it took a movie to make it from the theaters onto our black-and-white television set. My father's books were all nonfiction volumes on art, jazz, wine, or horse racing. There was no order to the shelves, so any time my mother wanted to find something like her paperback edition of *Wallflower at the Orgy*, she had to scan each row carefully, lest she miss it squeezed between a huge photographic history of bebop and an instructional guide to pace handicapping.

Our bookshelves were also lined with my mother's *tchotchkes*, which mocked the intellectual import of the books themselves. A plastic Kool-Aid man sat with his legs hanging off the edge of one shelf. Next to him stood *Star Trek*'s Captain Kirk with his phaser drawn, pointing at a perfectly preserved package of pink-coconut Hostess Sno-Balls that looked as plastic as their wrapping. On the next shelf up a pink glass flamingo whose base read "Greetings from Miami" stood perched on one leg, separating Mr. Spock and a stuffed Porky Pig, who seemed to be glaring at each other, ready to brawl. Interspersed among all these plastic and rubber toys were musty, handmade voodoo dolls that my mother had brought back from Haiti.

My mother had also nailed hooks into the wooden shelves and hung off them such items as a fake feather boa, an official 1970 census taker's bag, and several polling signs that read "Vote Here," "Vote Aqui," or words to the same effect in Asian languages. Amid this potpourri, the books themselves lost any intellectually intimidating sense they may have possessed and instead blended into the mishmash of cultural products and one-liners. Little did I know my own parents had plenty of the trappings of class that Michael's did; the signs were just hidden by all the knickknacks. In fact, the ironic kitsch of the menagerie itself was a form of cultural elitism.

The books in Michael's house evinced a different feeling. They smelled old and mildewy, and they were bound in leather, which had its own odor. In short, they smelled like something animate rather than something stamped out by a machine. Whereas we had a one-volume *New Columbia Encyclopedia*, they had a twenty-five-volume *Britannica*. My mother read constantly, and her reading was experiential. Whenever she read to me, the characters seemed to punch through the plastic cover of the library edition and rise to life, as if my mother had uttered an incantation. By contrast, at Michael's house reading was a means to an end, a way of finding something out. The words sat heavily in rows, as if still carrying the weight of the lead that had been used to typeset them; though the books were alive—they appeared to take a deep, labored breath with every turn of the page—their contents were dead. In fact, the entire house seemed like a museum. In addition to a piano, the Holts had a harpsichord that Michael and his brother played with ease. The ceilings in their home were the height of a cathedral and had exposed beams and a skylight, contrasting with the eight-foot-high, smooth cement ceilings that hung over my family like a heavy burden.

But for all these positive influences crammed into Michael's house, something there didn't hold together. No one got angry there, as they did at home when I would make my sister cry. My father would come barreling down the hallway, mad that I had interrupted his efforts to get some painting done, and knock me across the room with a fist against my shoulder. There was no corporal punishment at Michael's house. Even when he did something wrong, it all seemed play-acted.

"I poured the shampoo down the sink," Michael confessed one afternoon when we tried to concoct a special cleansing material to get the marker stains off of our backpacks. Before his mother could say anything, he would ask, "Am I grounded, or is my allowance docked?" This act of honesty appeared merely ritualistic to me, canned confession and punishment delivered with the aura that pervades the criminal justice system of an oppressive dictatorship where the outcome is always prefigured. There was no secret pleasure in sneaking a swig of soda or taking quarters from the laundry supply, and there was no Jewish guilt to follow it. Michael was, in fact, Jewish, although he and his family were blondish and followed none of the stereotypical social norms associated with Jewish life. Michael's older brother Danny even got to smoke pot in the house. When I asked his mother why she let him, she replied, as if the answer were obvious: "He's going to do what he wants anyway; I'd rather it be in the relative safety of our home than in some park with the police or junkies harassing him."

Honesty and household morality were such a given that the Holts could move on to a more ambitious agenda. They often went to, spoke at, and even organized political rallies, and not just in the P.S. 41 schoolyard. Since the Vietnam War was over and the Equal Rights Amendment had gone down to defeat, the cause du jour had become "No Nukes." I trucked out to Long Island with them and hundreds of thousands of other white people to protest the opening of an atomic power plant in Shoreham. I remember noticing the absence of any black, Hispanic, or Asian people. In fact, the entire event was so antithetical to my neighborhood's aesthetic that I flushed with embarrassment imagining what my friends from the projects would think.

Back in the projects gender differences were accentuated by push-up bras on the women and tight Lee jeans on the men. Here, by contrast, gender ebbed and flowed like the Brownian movement of bacteria in a puddle. Men had long hair and wore dresses and strings of beads, while women had hairy armpits and legs. People tried to get high by sniffing the tailpipe of a lavender-colored, gasohol-powered school bus. They played bongo drums and danced naked, their thick, loose skin flapping like garments. The decline of the hippie civilization was evident; the clan of tie-dyed protesters had the feel of a dying sect that could not recruit new members but had to enlarge its numbers from within. The few kids in attendance held onto their parents' legs as they stood around chatting, and the youngest sucked on mothers' milk, unperturbed by the half-million or so souls who milled about them.

As we passed by, one of the nursing mothers spoke to us. "How about a joint?" she asked. "Or some spare change?"

"I have no coinage or marijuana," Mr. Holt replied, "but here." He reached into his wallet and gave the woman a dollar. When others saw the flash of cash, they flocked to him as if he were the gasohol bus—or the girl with the Dunkin' Donuts. He handed a crisp dollar to everyone until his wallet was empty.

I looked away from these panhandlers, who seemed fake to me. Not even the poorest of souls from my neighborhood ever begged. Even the drunks who hung around outside the bullet-proofed liquor store on the corner of Pitt Street never asked for change. Besides, in their whiteness these panhandlers seemed like the privileged ones of society, not the needy. In my life, which contrasted minority, poor home neighborhood with rich, white school district, race and class had overlapped to such a great extent that it was difficult for me to separate poverty from dark skin color or to entertain the possibility of impoverished whites. Furthermore, though I couldn't pinpoint why, it didn't seem right to panhandle at a political rally. In fact, the whole reason for this huge gathering seemed lost in the on-the-ground interactions. Nuclear power in general and the Shoreham plant in particular seemed incidental, like the worthy charity benefited by a society dinner that everyone attends in order to be seen, rather than out of commitment to the cause. Since starting at P.S. 41, I had never been as happy to get home to my neighborhood as I was after that "No Nukes" rally.

Meanwhile, Michael and his parents were starting to wonder why I never invited him over to my house. They knew that I lived in a rough neighborhood and that it was dangerous for me to go home after dark, which was why I slept over once or twice a week. But they didn't understand why I never returned the gesture. The reason was twofold. First, I was ashamed of my neighborhood; second, I was embarrassed about Michael. Though he knew so many things, he was rather helpless in other ways. He still put on all his shirts and coats by laying them out across a flat surface, like his bed, and then crouching over to slip an arm through each sleeve before flipping the garment over his head. He also walked strangely, bouncing up and down with each step. I watched his heels carefully, trying to determine whether they actually touched the ground when he glided across the concrete. Everyone at home would snap all over him; they'd take one look at his long hair and call us gay. I simply couldn't be seen with him. The poor folks of my neighborhood had a certain wisdom, a certain street cachet that Michael and the others at school would never attain.

After a while, my own mother joined the chorus by asking why I never had Michael over on Thursday night, her designated kids' night, when she made pizza and let us each invite someone to stay over. Since I had transferred schools, I hadn't had anyone over to spend the night. I merely sat and growled as my sister and her friend enjoyed themselves, smearing tomato sauce on each other, playing house, or just giggling over nothing at all.

"Why don't you have your friend Michael come over this week?" she asked me on more than one occasion.

"Because," I always answered.

"Because why?" Our conversation had the rehearsed rhythm of a knock-knock joke.

"Because I don't want to, all right?" I shot back like a poison dart. "It's a free country, isn't it?"

"Is it because you're embarrassed of our house?" she asked. "Tell me, is there anything I can do to make it okay?"

I just sulked. It wasn't the apartment that I was ashamed of so much as the area that surrounded it. I wished I could have put up a board on the bottom half of all of our windows in order to block out the view of the immediate ten-block area, with its tenement fires and pigeon flocks. Often I would stare out the window, holding one hand up to shield my eye from the urban blight around us, looking only at our beautiful view of the Manhattan skyline. Then there was the walk from the bus stop to my front door. I normally crawled through the back fence, stepping over the broken glass, used syringes, and condoms that littered the space between the cluster of buildings and the junior high school behind them. There was no way that I could expose Michael to that.

I was also learning that the rules of class authority weren't as simple as they first appeared. When I imagined taking Michael out of the Village and bringing him to Avenue D, the entire dynamic got twisted up like an Escher bottle; there was no definite inside or outside anymore. I saw that poor people could wield authority over the nonpoor in certain face-to-face, local interactions, as a sort of consolation prize for the dominance the latter group exercised in the society as a whole. The fear that most whites experienced at night, walking alone on an empty street or alongside a minority pedestrian, formed part of these just deserts. As a white boy in the neighborhood, I already occupied a precarious enough social position; I didn't want to completely erode my legitimacy by traipsing home with Michael, someone who embodied liberal, middle-class values better than anyone else I knew.

But at last I gave in and invited Michael to come over the following week. Starting that day, I took the front way home from the bus stop, walking through the main entrance to the project even though it was out of my way. I picked up litter on each trip and scanned the area for eyesores that should and could be avoided. Empty malt liquor bottles appeared human-sized. Wrappers blew across my path like huge tumbleweeds, and I saw graffiti that I had never noticed before. Taking the front route home would avoid the most graffiti-ridden walls but expose Michael to more of the local kids hanging out in the playground. It also meant more steps with his heels not touching the ground and his long hair flapping up and down. I had never faced such a double-embarrassment bind before.

My anti-litter efforts were for naught. When Michael and I got off the bus that afternoon, it was clear the area around my house did not receive high priority from the New York City Department of Sanitation, even though we lived only two blocks from one of its main terminals. An entire fleet of garbage trucks sat parked right underneath the Williamsburg

Bridge, yet there had been no scheduled pickup that week. Black bags of garbage were stacked against the walls of all of the buildings, their contents bursting out into the streets. Not thinking about the fact that the Sanitation Department should have given us the same pick-up service that Greenwich Village received, I suddenly got angrier at all my neighbors than I had ever been. It was their fault that this place was a mess, I decided. And then, as if it were the next logical step, I concluded that it was even their fault that they were poor. I decided I would never be poor when I grew up.

As if beckoned by my angry thoughts, in that moment a hawk descended into the housing complex. I have a clearer memory of this scene than of the time when the SWAT team came to free hostages from the local pharmacy or when blue-uniformed policemen flooded the projects after a cop was shot in the elevator of the next building. Perhaps I remember it so well because Michael's presence had heightened my senses, my entire consciousness of my surroundings.

"*Media*, mommy, *águila*!" one little kid said as he tugged on his mother's hand, calling the bird an eagle. I remember her shooing away his chubby hand and checking her long red fingernails for damage; but then she, too, got caught up in the spectacle of the majestic bird that had entered our lives.

"No, no," she corrected her son. "*El azor*."

Soon everybody in the central courtyard area noticed the creature; people even watched from windows as the hawk plucked the carcass of a turkey out of one of the Hefty trash bags lined up against the Dumpster. As far as I could remember, it was the first time that everyone in the projects was silent at the same time. No one moved as the bird flapped its long wings for balance, wrestling the turkey out of the bag. The only problem was that after that day, lots of people left out half-eaten pork roasts, chickens, and anything else they thought would attract the huge bird of prey back to Avenue D. Meanwhile, I saw this as my opportunity. "Quick," I said as I tugged on Michael's arm, trying to take advantage of the distraction to sneak him up to my apartment unnoticed. "Let's go."

"Wait," he resisted my pull. "Look at that." He had not been staring at the hawk at all but was, in fact, facing a different direction, staring at another mound of garbage—a pile of broken old stereos and electronic parts. Before I could rope him in and guide him home, he had escaped to the heap of transistors and capacitors and was kneeling as he rummaged through the components. "We can make a radio out of this stuff," he cried out in joy. "Or even a transmitter!"

Some other kids came over. "Yo, you know how to do electronics?" Sean, the biggest one in the group, asked Michael.

"Yeah, we do." I interjected. We had recently given up coin collecting for electronics. Michael's parents had bought him a 150-in-1 project kit from Radio Shack, and on our Tuesday afternoons we had built a series of chirping machines and crystal radios and even a crude calculator. He was better at it than I was. On the days I didn't sleep over his house, I sat up working out possible circuits on paper, but without the kit, I couldn't test them, and they usually failed the next Tuesday. I had never thought to salvage any of the many carcasses of televisions, radios and other electrically-powered wares that littered my streets.

"Can you make me a laser?" Sean asked, still looking at Michael.

"Yes," I promised. "We can make you a laser . . . "

"No," Michael cut off my efforts at assimilation with the truth. "We don't have the capabilities to construct a laser."

"Yo," Sean spat out of a twisted-up mouth. "Why you got to lie, punk?" He slapped at my head with a force that was somewhere between playful and violent.

"That's awright, man," he said to Michael. "Thanks anyways."

I strained muscles in my face that I didn't know I had in order to hold back my tears. Michael had outdone me in my own neighborhood.

After the day of the hawk, Michael slept over fairly regularly on Thursday nights throughout fourth and fifth grades. I had swallowed my embarrassment over the laser interaction with Sean and grew less and less ashamed of my surroundings. I still faced the problem of money, however. Class I could fake to some extent, like I did with *antidisestablishmentarianism*, but money there was no finessing. Each Tuesday I swallowed my hungry fast-food cravings when Michael and I and whomever else he had invited promenaded around the Village, entertaining ourselves for a while before going to his house. Michael suggested that we all get a slice at Ray's, then walk down to the doughnut shop for some of those delicacies that had helped insure Jimmy Carter's schoolyard victory. When Michael saw that I wasn't eating at Ray's, he held out his slice and offered, "Do you want to try some?"

"No, I'm not hungry," I said, though I could barely stand to look on as they competed to see who could stretch the cheese the longest from the pizza to his mouth. My family wasn't so poor that my parents couldn't have given me a dollar or two a week for snacks. The main reason I had no cash was philosoph-ical: my parents simply didn't believe in spending money on junk food. Even in my own neighborhood, where I already knew I was better off than most of my peers, I felt I was the only one who couldn't participate in the ritual of consump-tion. The other kids always seemed to have money for an icie when the one-eyed man rolled into the area with his wooden cart and big block of ice. All the children would whip folded dollar bills out of their sneakers or dig up some change from secret pockets in their sundresses. I always stood and watched as the old street hawker scraped up a coneful, asking each cus-tomer in Spanish which *sabor*, which flavor, he or she wanted. One day the ice-cream truck rolled up Rivington Street with its siren song of refreshment, and I could resist no longer. I ripped out the emergency transportation money my mother had taped under the insole of my sneaker. With that creased, sweaty dollar bill I purchased a large soft-serve cone dipped in rainbow sprinkles.

The next week, on my Tuesday afternoon with Michael, I lifted the insole of my *other* shoe and removed the mugging money my mother had placed there, a ten-dollar bill that I was supposed to hand over politely to satisfy an assailant. I spent two bucks on pizza and soda and divided the change among my two shoes: seven dollars for the mugger, one dollar to replace the emergency bus fare I had torn out the week be-fore. I did this as surreptitiously as I could, as to not catch the notice of the others. Then we stopped by the science fiction shop, and I spent the remaining eight dollars on a stack of comic books, rationalizing that I could give them to a mugger instead of the money.

I grew addicted to purchasing. I had never realized how empowering it felt to spend money. Free monetary exchange was so liberating—until the cash ran out. Then I cracked. It was a school holiday, and a bunch of neighborhood kids and I were in the local combination candy store–luncheonette. I was reading comic books at the rack, having discovered that there existed an infinite number of comic books that I needed to own—far more than eight dollars' worth. Suddenly, the free exchange of goods seemed oppressive. I became overwhelmed by the volume of things for sale. And they just kept coming. I would never be able to keep up with all the material goods that could be purchased and consumed.

Earl and the other Mini School kids were busy loading up on sugar. They bought Mike and Ikes. They got Now and Laters. They even purchased a type of candy that was pure sugar, flavored vaguely to resemble various fruits and packaged in straws; they sucked this powder up into their mouths as if snorting cocaine orally. Even better were the bags of this processed sugar, sold with a spoon that itself was made of solid sugar. I could resist all these temptations, but chocolate I could not. Reggie Bar, a new product named after Yankee slugger Reggie Jackson, had just hit the market. It consisted of a blob of chocolate and nuts that looked like it was just shot out of a machine and had gelled instantly into whatever random shape. I had to have one. While the cashiers were ringing up the other kids, I rushed out the door, a stolen comic book and two Reggie Bars in hand.

I ate my candy greedily in the playground, reading the Silver Surfer comic while the other kids inhaled their sugar. The group of us then rode the glucose wave, running around the complex madly, playing ring-a-levio and tag and terrorizing younger children by taking their Big Wheels for joy rides. Within an hour my head throbbed, and I crawled off to my house. There I found my mother reclining on the burlap sofa, watching television with a wet washcloth on her head. She must have had a migraine herself. Phil Donahue was on the screen, ranting about something, as I came up to her and complained that I had a headache.

The guilt I felt over having stolen from the nice couple who ran the store matched the pain in my head; in fact, in that moment it seemed to be the cause of the pressure that I felt against my temples. My mother must have seen something in my eyes, or maybe she simply noticed the comic book I was clutching, but she immediately questioned me through the haze of her own headache.

"You had candy, didn't you?" she asked.

I nodded. I only wanted sympathy, no matter what I had to admit.

"You spent your emergency shoe money, didn't you?" she asked, her voice dropping in tone and becoming sterner. I nodded again. Evidently her powers of maternal ESP ended there, since she didn't ask me any more questions. "You'll have to work off the money," she said. Then she laid me down on the carpeted floor, wetting a washcloth for me and feeding me a generic Tylenol with a glass of water. We lay there, watching from Phil on through the evening news. My headache was still there. By now I was convinced that I had to confess everything in order to gain relief.

"That's not all," I said, as if our conversation of a couple hours before were continuing uninterrupted. "I—I . . . " Unable to get out the words, I started crying. Suddenly I was flooded with the images of the proprietors' faces, looking at me through baggy eyes like dogs in a pound. They must have been shy of fifty years old at the time, but they were gray-haired and seemed ancient to me. The image of them led me to dwell on the old men who sat along Delancey Street a few blocks west, selling shoelaces. I remembered how my mother said that was how they made their living, one shoelace at a time. Then I remembered her pointing out to me an old woman buying cat food in the supermarket. She bent over and whispered in my ear, "She probably doesn't have cats."

"How do you know she doesn't have cats?" I had responded, a little too loudly. Luckily the woman in question was almost deaf or faked it by not reacting.

"Social Security isn't enough for many old people," she explained, again in a whisper, "so they can't afford regular food." I had no idea what Social Security was at the time, but I did notice a remarkable drop in the number of old people buying animal food and selling shoelaces over the course of the next few years. I assumed they were all dead. Only later did I learn that Nixon had instituted a series of generous cost-of-living increases in Social Security, lifting many seniors out of poverty. I felt a sympathy for the elderly poor that I never had for children my own age, and in my aching head that day my theft was directly linked to the plight of the cat-food eaters and shoelace salesmen.

"I stole from the luncheonette," I finally sputtered. My headache didn't go away as I had thought it would. In fact, confessing didn't make me feel better at all.

"You *stole?*" my mother asked, as if she needed to hear it out of her own mouth in order to believe it. "You stole from the luncheonette? *Our* luncheonette?"

The clamp on my head seemed to ratchet tighter as I sensed that my punishment was going to go beyond a simple, Michael Holt–style penance such as grounding or extra chores. Sure enough, my mother instructed, "Well you're just going to have to go down there, return it, and apologize to them."

"I already ate it," I said, confessing this additional sin in the hopes that the lack of physical evidence might thwart her plan.

"What was it?" she asked.

"A Reggie Bar," I explained. "Okay, two."

"Let's go," she said.

"No," I wailed, trying to wriggle out of the grip she had on my wrist. "They're gone," I remember saying. "There's nothing to return."

"Then you'll have to give them back the money."

"I don't have any money," I shot back, strangely satisfied at my ability to come up with one excuse after another.

"I'm going to lend you the money." Her grip got tighter. I could feel the arteries in my wrist, pulsing out of sync with the ones that throbbed in my head.

"I don't wanna go," I said, still trying to twist away. My hand was turning purple and puffy; it felt as if someone were taking my blood pressure.

She let my arm drop, but I knew I had no choice. The mesmerizing command of her gaze was more forceful than her grip had been. She marched me out of the apartment and down to the luncheonette. In the elevator, she dug through her purse, asking me how much candy bars cost. "Thirty cents each!" she exclaimed upon learning. After going through the entire contents of her bag, rummaging through crumpled Kleenexes and melted, fused Lifesavers, she found a quarter and enough nickels to pay the proprietors without having to break a bill.

When we arrived my mother pushed me up to the register like a stage mother urging her child to perform. Behind the counter stood the woman, whom somehow I preferred dealing with over her husband. I unfurled my fist to reveal the silver coins and dropped them onto the spiked, black rubber mat that sat on the counter next to the cash register. I still could not look into the woman's eyes, staring instead at the faded blue numbers tattooed on the inside of her arm. Some of the coins were so dirty and sweaty that they remained stuck to my palm, and I had to shake them off before the full sixty cents had been presented for acceptance. Then I felt my mother's hand at my back again. This time she pricked me with her fingernails.

"Dalton has something to tell you," she said when I still hadn't spoken.

"Um . . . ," I said. I knew I was supposed to confess my

crime, but my mother and I had not negotiated exactly what I would say. "Um . . . I stoled something from you." Now I no longer even looked at the tattoo but rather stared straight down at the ground. "I stoled two things."

"I see," she said in her Yiddish accent. "You know, you could go to jail for vat you did."

I didn't say anything. I thought only of the comic book, which I had not yet confessed to stealing.

"Tell me vy I should not have you in jail?" she asked. "Vat have you learned from this?"

"I learned that . . . ," I started to say, as if beginning to recite the Pledge of Allegiance. It felt as though I were spouting off multiplication tables or state capitals, something I was supposed to know by rote. Suddenly it didn't feel like I had learned anything at all—except, perhaps, that I could just as easily have lied about the Reggie Bars as I had about the comic book. In that moment my desire to repent evaporated, and I grew resentful that this woman and my mother had taken such a heavy tone and Socratic approach with me. They were merely trying to coax out the goodness at my moral core, but the actual truth was that I was continuing to lie—at least, I was withholding information. I had stolen an item even more valuable than the candy—and was getting away with it. This is what I learned.

"Let me tell you a story," the woman said. I was praying that none of the Piratas baseball players would walk in and see me there with my mother, actually talking to the luncheonette lady everyone ridiculed.

"When I was a young girl in Germany in the concentration camp"—and as her tone of voice changed I perked up and listened, sensing that, lie or no lie, now I might really learn something—"my family and I were being marched off to the gas chambers." She paused. I had heard about the Nazis before, both in school and from my mother in connection with Martin, the German foster child who had lived with her family for several months. "I was only a young girl of twelve," she continued, "but we had all heard about the showers and ovens, so we knew we were going to die."

I couldn't stand still; it felt as if something would drop on my head if I stayed in one place. I wanted to escape but knew I had no choice but to stay and listen. I fidgeted and rocked back and forth on my feet, dreading the story but also fascinated by it, as if it were a dead animal I had found in the gutter and was poking with a stick. I was both disturbed and enthralled by its ugliness.

"I had nothing to lose, so I ran up to one of the guards," she continued. "I looked him right in the eye and said, 'We all have to die some time, and it may be sooner for me than for you, but at least I'll be able to face my Jewish God when that time comes. What about you? Can you face your God?'"

My eyes met hers, just as she had met the gaze of the guard. Her big blue irises had a liquid glaze over them. "Do you know vat he did?" she asked me. "Do you know vat this guard did?" She didn't wait for an answer. The Socratic part of this lesson was over. "He pulled me out of the line and saved my life. Everyone else in my family was killed. All my brothers and sisters and my parents, too." Now she was crying, as was I. "But I spoke up for my beliefs, and God spared me." Then she turned to my mother. "It is because of this, I say, you have to raise them Jewish. You're raising him Jewish?" she asked, the upward lilt returning to her voice.

I was glad that the moral spotlights of her eyes were off me and on my mother. I reran her story in my mind as she spoke to my mother about the importance of keeping the Jewish faith alive. "Why?" I asked suddenly. I had worked through the story and arrived at what I thought were its logical implications: namely, that being Jewish generally led to execution. "Does she want us all to get killed?"

My mother gasped and grabbed me by the ear, twisting the cartilage, yanking me toward the door. "I apologize," she said to the woman as I wailed. "I'm so sorry. Please forgive us."

When we got home, my mother locked me in my room for the rest of the evening. The next day she revealed my punishment. To work off the money I had taken from my shoe and the cost of the Reggie Bars, I would perform a series of household chores. For three weeks I vacuumed the carpet, scrubbed the bathroom, and did the laundry in the basement. This paid off eight dollars, and I was forgiven the difference. Strangely enough, I was thrilled to have earned my own money, and I asked my parents if I could work for money all the time. We negotiated a list of chores and fees ranging from twenty-five cents for vacuuming the floor once a week to two dollars for doing the family laundry. I had the potential to earn about three dollars and fifty cents per week. From then on, this is how I spent my Friday nights. Three-fifty was just enough money to let me buy a snack in the Village on Tuesday afternoon, with a little left over for when I was hanging out with the local kids. My theft had worked out for the best. Instead of repeating it, I was channeled into the world of work.

But, like the ice-cream cone that had started my run of illicit purchases, the money I earned at home only served to whet my financial appetite. I could now hang out with Michael at Ray's Pizza and be part of the group, but I soon developed new needs that required even more money. So one day in fifth grade I walked into Candy Kisses, a store that stood around the corner from P.S. 41. Candy Kisses was nothing like the luncheonette, whose rack of treats flanked the register, sandwiched by newspapers on one side and a paltry selection of cigars on the other. Candy Kisses had none of the brand-name items I knew and craved: no SweeTarts or Hot Tamales, no Gobstoppers or Jawbreakers. The store didn't offer candy so much as confections. It sold hunks of chocolate individually wrapped in clear plastic with pink bows, even chocolate in a white color that amazed me. There were hard candies shaped like flowers, lips, or ducklings. The store even carried marzipan, which baffled and intimidated me.

Usually I just browsed there during my lunch hour. The prices at Candy Kisses were beyond the reach of my three-fifty budget; only the kids who got ten-dollar allowances bought from this purveyor. But on this particular occasion, I hung around after all the other kids had filtered out, returning to school with their delicacies. I asked the proprietor whether he needed any help. He hired me to work during my lunch hour, stacking boxes and keeping an eye on the droves of kids to make sure they weren't stealing anything. He paid me five dollars a week and gave me an employee discount on all items in the store. Soon he bestowed a raise upon me, and my combined weekly income from home and the labor market broke into the double digits. I thought I finally made enough money to rank among the leaders in disposable income in my class. Then I heard that the Dunkin' Donuts girl and a couple of others had gotten raises as well in the inflation-ridden era of the late 1970s. Their allowances now stood at twenty dollars a week. I would never be able to keep up, it seemed.

Soon after that my mother received a telephone call from my principal, who had gotten wind of my lunch-hour employment. "Isn't it terrible?" he asked my mother rhetorically. "Using child labor during school hours. I'm sure you weren't aware of this; that's why I wanted to bring it to your attention. I've contacted the establishment and warned them that they better terminate his employment or face prosecution."

"Mmm hmm," she replied as she swallowed a piece of Godiva chocolate I had brought her on payday. "Thank you for your concern. Thank you very much." She hung up the phone and cursed the loss of her discounted chocolate.

If I had already learned about class distinctions in my first two years of commuting across town, now I was being taught the contradictions and ironies of class mobility. Having been taught not to steal by my mother and the luncheonette woman, I was now being told it was not okay to work for money, either. The easiest solution, it seemed, might be to return to theft. But my mother, perhaps sensing my frustration, told me she would find another job for me. Unlike most of our neighbors, whose parents had little in the way of useful social connections, my mother could make good on her promise. Through one of her friends, she soon found me a job sweeping out the Ukrainian meeting hall on Second Avenue. The pay for one afternoon of work was the same as I made for the entire week of lunch hours at Candy Kisses. But the glamour of white chocolate was gone.

Just as I commuted each school day from a poor, minority section of New York to a white, upper-middle-class area, so did I travel each summer with my family to white-as-could-be, middle-class Pennsylvania. My sister and I went under duress. We longed to spend the summers in New York, when the sprinklers in the playground were turned on and kids would come streaming out of their stuffy apartments wearing bathing suits, making beelines for the metallic mushroom spouting water in the central courtyard. Instead, Alexandra and I had to swim in a cold artesian lake. Even though I dreaded Pennsylvania, I knew that going to the country was considered a luxury and that there were even special programs like the Fresh Air Fund that tried to give my neighbors a taste of it. So I never mentioned this annual vacation to anyone in the projects and just disappeared quietly at the end of each June. Across town, however, I played it up, knowing that leaving New York in summer was part of the status game that went on at school. But I withheld the fact that sometimes we stayed in a tent and other times we lived in a small cottage that belonged to a friend of my mother.

Though this summer foray scored me some points in the Village, there was nothing about our annual routine that I dreaded more. For me, the end of June—just before we left New York, but after school let out—was the only time I felt whole. For a week or two I didn't have to live a split life between school and home, and I could hang out with my neighborhood peers and repair those friendships. By far the worst part about going to Pennsylvania was that it forced me to quit the Little League team I had worked so hard to earn a place on. Las Piratas were one of the best teams in the Lower East Side league, and securing a spot on the roster was no easy feat. I never felt more a part of the community than I did with the Piratas.

But every season without fail, just as my bat was heating up and the bigger kids were starting to show me some respect, my parents would yank me off the team and out of New York City. After the first couple of years the coach caught on to the pattern, knowing that I always left the team in the middle of the season and missed the playoffs. So, despite my good batting average, in 1980 he gave my starting outfield slot to Peaches, a Puerto Rican kid who got his name from his rosy complexion. I continued to play for the Piratas as a reserve, however, and so stayed connected to some of the project kids with whom I no longer attended school.

It didn't even have to be organized play. One late-June afternoon, before we were to leave for Pennsylvania, I caught sight from my room of a Spalding baseball game taking shape down below, in the glass-littered Hamilton Fish Park behind our building. It looked as if the game was about to start, so instead of waiting for the unreliable elevators I raced down the entire twenty-one flights of stairs. I crawled through the fence that separated the project from the park, but the game had already begun. "Yo," I said when I got to the cement baseball diamond. "Lemme sub in?" I spoke differently here from how I did across town. "I got a glove," I added as an enticement. Many of the kids could not afford gloves, so they either played at a disadvantage with bare hands or borrowed one from someone on the other team. Mitts flying through the air from the lender to the borrower or vice versa always marked the end of each inning. With me in the game, one more kid could play with a glove.

"Get the fuck out of here, honky," said one of the captains, Sean. Despite his Irish name, Sean was Puerto Rican. He commanded a lot of respect in the neighborhood, for two reasons. First, he was about four inches taller than most of us, had filled out into a muscular frame, and did not hesitate to throw his weight around, against, or on top of us. The other factor that legitimated his leadership was that he had been on television. In fact, he was on TV practically every day, as part of the final credits for *Sesame Street*, riding a horse along with Big Bird as the numbers and letters that had sponsored that day's show scrolled over his tan, bare back. He had filmed this bit a few years earlier and received ninety-nine dollars for his appearance, or so he said. Ninety-nine dollars made him the richest kid in the group, in addition to the biggest.

Just as I was about to slink off, the kid who was the captain of the other team piped up in my defense. "He's good," said Angel, who knew me from the Piratas. "We'll take him on our team." That day I played well, smacking the rubber ball over the rightfield fence twice for home runs that helped our victory. Afterward I asked James, the kid on the other team who used my mitt, for my glove back.

"No," he said. "I'm keeping it."

"Say what?" I asked.

"It's my glove," he repeated. He was a very thin, dark-skinned kid who towered over everyone, even Sean.

"That's cold," said Peaches, my Piratas replacement.

"Come on, man." I said, reaching out with my hand. I sized up my chances in a fight. Though James was tall, he was all bones and joints and looked as if his knees and elbows were tree knots.

"Come on *what?*" James asked rhetorically. He held his chin up, and his chest barreled out in a gesture of challenge. Normally adversaries would strut around in this position, jamming their chests into each other, but given our height disparity, the breast of his sweaty tank top was stuffed in my face. Typically, each provocateur would pin back his arms, since any contact with the hands would mean that a fight had actually begun, and the truth was that usually no one really wanted to fight at all. Most of these confrontations ended peacefully, if not amicably; friends would intervene, and the parties usually walked away cussing at each other, turning back with a threat after every other step.

In this case, however, my choice became clear: I could avoid a fight but forfeit my glove, or I could attack James and hope to win. I had no idea what chance I stood in such a confrontation. I had not gotten into a fight in the neighborhood for a couple of years, not since the day I wore my karate outfit down to the playground despite my mother's warning.

James held the glove aloft, his outstretched arm well beyond my reach. I tried to yank it down when chaos descended. I found myself pulled away from James, my arms twisted more than halfway out of their sockets as if I were the Barbie doll being fought over at Head Start years earlier. My chin banged against an elbow as someone crushed my throat with the full might of his biceps. Then, just as I was trying to remember the move Rahim had taught me to get out of this hold, I felt the coolness of a blade up against my neck. In contrast to the hot fleshiness that gripped me and my own balmy skin, the stainless steel of the knife felt unmistakable. While the rest of us had been tossing our mitts to each other between innings, Sean and a couple of other Junior Outlaws had been showing off their new switchblades, competing to see who could arm himself the quickest.

Even James seemed shocked at the turn of events. "Damn!" he said, the arm that held the mitt in question falling limp at his side.

"Should I slice the honky?" Sean asked.

I squirmed like an animal being readied for butchering—mute, uncomfortable, and not quite aware enough to be terrified.

"Should I cut him?"

Angel was nowhere to be seen. In fact, everyone was eerily quiet as Sean laughed, his cackle sounding like that of a listener scared by a ghost story. It dawned on me that no one, least of all me, was quite sure what was going on or exactly what Sean's intentions were. Much to my own amazement, I was not particularly scared. Instead I took in the whole scene—the surprise on everyone's face, their rapt attention—with the same curiosity Sean must have experienced as he looked around. It almost felt as if we were a team, a vaudeville act, rather than perpetrator and victim. Then, as if I had suddenly woken up from what I thought had been a dream only to discover that I was caught in another layer of nightmare, I realized that I was in a potentially dangerous situation. There was absolutely nothing I could do. I was not strong enough to wriggle free and I could barely speak for want of air, so I could not bargain with my aggressor. All I could do was try to restrain the crushing force of his forearm on my trachea by wrapping both hands around his wrist bone and pulling with all my strength, as if I were attempting a chin-up. As I struggled, there was a silence like that which descended when the hawk flew into the housing complex. This quietude scared me more than anything else, for something must have truly been amiss for that snapping, hollering bunch to fall mute.

I felt Sean press the blade harder against my neck, seemingly needing to push things one step further to get a rise out of the group. "Check it out, y'all," he said as he stood more erect, lifting me with him, onto my tiptoes. He swung me from left to right and back again, making me dance like a marionette. On top of the coat of dried-out sweat from the game, I now had a filmy layer of nervous perspiration; oilier and more viscous, it acted as my only defense against the knife, causing the blade to slide around. It was as if I were getting my first, raw shave, my red throat feeling more like it had been sunburned than sliced.

Finally, as I danced around on my tiptoes, Sean got the response he was looking for: chuckles from the crowd. Peaches spoke up first. "*Mira*, Sean, you are the baddest nigger around," he said.

"He real scared," Tito added. I might as well not have been present; they spoke matter-of-factly, as if everything had already gone down. At first this apparent disregard of my existence made me more fearful than had the silence that preceded it. But after the initial drop in my stomach, I realized this was the other kids' way of managing the crisis. My pleading with Sean would only have provoked him, made it more of a show in which he had to press the knife tighter and tighter against my neck in order to build up to some climactic event—one that could only have been bad news for me. Tito and Peaches, by speaking as if the situation and I were long over, as if everything were fact and not contingency, were tacking a premature denouement onto the scene, one that would lead to my imminent release.

Still, Sean did not let go. Only a few seconds later, when he heard a siren go by on Houston Street, did he drop me from his grasp. "Damn," he said when he heard the police car speed by. "Five-O."

"Five-O," everyone yelled in response. The police siren was far away and obviously not headed in our direction, as the Doppler shift—the rise and fall in its tone—revealed. It faded off toward the West Side, never coming close to our makeshift baseball diamond. Though never any real threat, the squad car had given Sean his out, a socially acceptable reason to let me go, an excuse for having drawn his weapon but not having drawn blood. He and the other Junior Outlaws flipped up the collars on their windbreakers in some sort of appropriation of 1950s gang behavior. They wore these outer layers despite the humid June weather. As the rest scattered Sean folded up his knife, displaying a lot less ease and agility than he had in drawing the weapon. Before racing off with the other kids he turned and winked at me, as if it were the end of that day's episode of Sesame Street. Then he, too, crawled through the hole in the fence and was gone.

I sat where he had dropped me from his grip, my palms bloody from having broken my fall. I stared at the flesh of my hands. The teeniest stones had wedged themselves into my skin, along with slivers of brown, green, and clear glass. My palms sported a perfect imprint of the surface on which they had landed, mirrored the imperfections in the gravel-based cement that had seemed so smooth from afar. Like the park surface itself, my palms glittered as the afternoon sun bounced off them. Sitting there, on the verge of tears, all I felt was sorry for myself. Only later would I realize that, given the racial geography of my childhood, it is surprising how little actual violence I encountered. I can't imagine that a black kid growing up in a poor white neighborhood would have gotten off so lightly.

I vowed never to play pickup ball in Hamilton Fish Park again. I was being separated—or separating myself—from my neighbors one game at a time: first manhunt, now baseball. So maybe it was fitting that I never got my glove back from James. I was never happier to be leaving for the summer than I was that afternoon, sitting there on the pitted cement. Only in retrospect did I realize that this episode with Sean was the best thing that could have happened to me. Had I been accepted by the group, had I become a gang member—first a Junior Outlaw, then a full-fledged Outlaw—perhaps all the commuting to school and summers in Pennsylvania would have made little difference, and my life chances might not have been that much better than those of the people around me. I'll never know whether it was my mother's protectiveness, my expectations and aspirations, or simply my race that spared me from a worse fate. I will never know the true cause and effect in the trajectory of my life. And maybe it is better that way. I can believe what I want to believe. This is the privilege of the middle and upper classes in America—the right to make up the reasons things turn out the way they do, to construct our own narratives rather than having the media and society do it for us.

Those first summers in Pennsylvania we camped out near enough to my grandparents' house that we could do our laundry and take showers there; after that one of my mother's few Jewish friends from her childhood in Carbondale lent us his cottage. We made our annual jaunts by packing everything we owned into the fifteen-year-old automobile we had received as a hand-me-down from my mother's parents. We would ride the huge black Oldsmobile luxury sedan through the Pocono Mountains, my sister and I splayed out across the blue silk car seats. We used to pretend we were riding a cruise ship, our fantasy aided by the glug-glug of the old Diet Pepsi bottles we kept filled with water for when the engine overheated. We fooled around with the lighted vanity mirrors, which whispered messages of class from a bygone era. We played with the electric windows and gazed into the glow of the dashboard as if it were the comforting hearth of a country fireplace.

In the late 1970s, northeastern Pennsylvania was already awash in department-store overstock, irregulars, and factory seconds of some of the world's best off-the-rack clothing

brands. The region had evolved into a center for factory out-
lets, to which busloads of retirees and bargain-hunters flocked
from all across the mid-Atlantic. It was a historical accident that
the twelve miles of Route 6 between Carbondale and Scranton
had developed into one of the first of the seemingly endless
chains of strip malls that today litter the American landscape.

While the great coal mining era of the United States wound
slowly down in the wake of World War II, in Carbondale it
ground to a sudden halt in 1959. That year the main mine collapsed, killing a dozen miners; their bodies remain trapped to
this day in the veins of anthracite that run beneath the town.
Meanwhile, a mine fire had been alternately raging and smoldering since the 1940s, its heat causing flowers to bloom in
winter. In 1972, a local entrepreneur with federal "urban
blight" financing finally put it out by filling the major caverns
of the mine with dirt and rocks pushed in from neighboring
land. In the process he peeled off the topsoil, inaugurating a
new epoch of strip mining. This method of coal retrieval took
a quick and heavy toll on the land, and after the stretch between Carbondale and Scranton had been taken for all the fos-
sil fuel it was worth, malls and plastic-shelled stores cropped
up there like weeds in a slag heap. And such was the local—
quite tangible—transformation from industrial to postindustrial economy—that is, from manufacturing to service, from
production to consumption, from local to global.

As we drove along Route 6 one year, I asked my parents
what the area produced to get all these stores in return. "I
mean, all these cars," I said, waving toward a new car lot. A

glint of afternoon light jumped from one new automobile to the next as we drove by them, as if some solar finger were individually blessing each new Chevrolet and its cash-back rebate or low-interest financing plan. "They don't come from here."

"What do you mean?" my father asked, turning quickly to make eye contact for a split second. His brow was wrinkled, his expression almost worried, as if what I was driving at upset him too, and he wanted to avoid the whole subject. But finally he shrugged and admitted, "Yeah, the cars come from Detroit or Japan."

My mother jumped in, sensing an underlying insult to her home community, her insecurities and sensitivities keying up with charge as if the ends of her frizzy hair were picking up something in the air. "They pay for their cars like anyone else," she said.

I leaned forward, draping myself over the back of the front seat, poking my head into the adult section. "They are getting the cars from somewhere, and they are getting all these clothes from somewhere; so what are they producing here that gets shipped out?"

"Retail," she said hurriedly, as if she sensed the tenuousness of her logic and wanted to get it out before it crumbled. "All these retail stores."

"Yeah," I insisted. "But they didn't make the things that sell here, so that's a loss too."

"They make metal grates and gas masks," she countered, seeming more worried than before, worried that if she herself could not figure out what sustained the local economy, it might collapse in that very moment. "And agriculture," she added, excited that she had thought of something else. "Corn and milk and cattle—"

I was about to interrupt her, shout that no quantity of gas masks or metal grates or ears of corn could pay for all the stuff that lined the highway, but my father jumped in first. "Manure!" he cried. "Night crawlers! Dirt!" he added to her litany. My sister was laughing now at the idea of selling dirt. But it was true; when we turned off Route 6 and headed on the backroads to the cottage, we always passed several signs advertising these products.

Even my mother got into the spirit, yelling out, "Babies! White babies!"

"That's right," my father smiled, as if she had reminded him of some fundamental axiom. Poor women got several thousand dollars to give up their newborns to rich city folk or to carry someone else's fertilized egg.

"Who'd want to buy the retards up here?" I said, hissing through my teeth. I slouched back in my seat, pouting, unconvinced that the region was paying off its trade deficit in fleshy pink babies.

"You're just so smug and superior, and I can't stand it!" my mother snapped, in a tone quite different from that she'd used a few moments earlier. "The people up here are good people who work for their money, and you are just such a—a—an *ass*," she said. This epithet shocked the entire family, most of all my mother herself. She almost never used profanity, and this was as close as she could get.

That summer's ride was more interesting than most, but once we arrived at the cottage my sister and I were bored to no end, pining to be back in the city. Not only were we bored, we were scared. The sign marking the entrance to the Commonwealth of Pennsylvania from neighboring New Jersey read, "Welcome to Pennsylvania: Where America Starts." My sister and I could not help but be intimidated by this America, with its single-family homes, aluminum siding, U.S. flags, and front-yard statues of Negro jockeys. We had no idea how to react when people we didn't know waved to us as they cruised by in their shiny cars. We didn't know what to say when someone on the dirt road that ran behind our cottage asked how we were doing. Such friendliness was not part of our America.

Given that this was her homeland, my mother had a personal stake in making my sister and me feel comfortable, so she encouraged us to assimilate into the local culture. At first she coaxed us into playing with the few other kids who lived nearby—one family in particular had children our age. Our friendship lasted only one afternoon, however, before we were exiled from that household on account of all the profanity we employed as part of our normal speech. We knew never to swear at anyone directly, but using cuss words in a sentence had seemed completely acceptable to us. The father of the two kids dropped us back at our cottage, apologizing the whole while to my mother, as if his refusal to expose his children to such language reflected some failing or cultural limitation on his part. After he left, my mother asked what bad words Alexandra and I had used, but neither of us could remember anything remarkable we had said and merely shrugged our shoulders. My father bothered the neighbors, too, with the loud reggae music he played in the cottage as he spray-painted his abstract forms onto canvas.

"Can you turn that down please?" my mother would ask him often, knowing that the car dealer who lived in the house next to ours would be too polite to ask my father himself.

"No, I cannot turn it fucking down," he would yell back in the ritualized exchange, before adding, "Dub it, mon!"

My mother would flinch, and my father would wink at me. We liked our music loud, as our neighbors did back on Avenue D. There we couldn't compete, however. Boom-box radios had just hit the market, and an arms race of sorts had developed in the projects. The neighborhood would just be starting to erupt with bass riffs as we left town each summer. Residents—men and teenage boys, primarily—were getting progressively bigger radios with more and more features, trying to outdo each other in the battle for control of the airspace. Even on the twenty-first floor, massive sub-woofers used to rattle our windows whenever someone walked by with the Sugar Hill Gang's "Rapper's Delight" or Anita Ward's "Ring My Bell" cranked up to maximum volume. Some people even bought portable systems with built-in record players, essentially carrying an entire stereo unit on their shoulder. The ability to sustain the weight of these enormous boxes became part of the competition. The silver behemoth and the music emanating from it announced to everyone around that, despite poverty and powerlessness, "Yo, I am here. You hear?" In northeastern Pennsylvania, by contrast, no one carried radios anywhere.

My mother's efforts at rural assimilation were not limited to turning down the volume of my father's music. After we failed to hit it off with the kids across the road, she made Alexandra attend a sleepover birthday party for the daughter of one of her old high school friends. At first Alexandra enjoyed herself, awed by the suburban splendor of the recreation room, with its deep-pile wall-to-wall carpeting and full bar. The birthday girl's father fixed everyone Shirley Temples with umbrellas and plastic-looking maraschino cherries, and the kids played pinball and Twister and baked Rice Krispie treats. When Alexandra went to the bathroom she was amazed at the bright blue splendor of the quilted toilet paper and the matching hue of the chlorine eddies that appeared each time she flushed the toilet.

Everything was going fine until it was time to hunker down for the night. All the girls formed a circle with their sleeping bags and told ghost stories. The first was about a girl whose head wasn't really attached to her body; the second was about Bigfoot; and the third told of a girl who strayed from her campsite and got lost in the woods. Owls hooted and wild animals growled, frightening the little girl.

"Then he appeared," the storyteller explained. "The huge nigger stumbled forward with a squirrel in one hand whose head he'd bitten off."

Alexandra thought she had misheard, but the tale continued: "The nigger took one look at the little girl and reached out with his claws to eat her." She spoke not with racial hatred but in the same tone with which the previous storyteller had described Bigfoot, as if blacks were fairy-tale characters. My sister's mind flashed to images of her dark-skinned friends back in New York and she considered speaking up, but instead she swallowed the dryness in her throat and tried to will herself to sleep for the night.

As Alexandra retold the story, she felt most ashamed of herself for having made a mental connection between the fictional "nigger" of the woods and her friends back in New York. Those friends used the term themselves, even called each other niggers, but they spoke the word with a sarcastic bite that negated its content. At any rate, the word never seemed dirty until we heard it used in the white Pennsylvania suburbs. Here, racism was expressed but apparently not thought much about; by contrast, I often reflected, on Avenue D it was often thought about but never spoken of—at least not directly to us.

Not too long after the sleepover, Alexandra had to attend summer school in Carbondale, where all but a handful of residents were Italian or Irish. She had enrolled in the world history course to make up for a class she had failed back in New York. "China," the teacher announced the first day of class, following the state-imposed curriculum, "China has one billion people," he said. "You know what that means?" Alexandra shook her head along with all the other kids in the class. The instructor continued, "That means two billion armpits and one billion assholes. On to the next country . . . " He sped this way across the globe before arriving safely back in Europe. "Everybody originates from Europe," he said. "No matter what anyone else says, man started in Europe, not Africa." He waved his arm over the class. "Is anyone's family not from Europe?" he asked, as if the issue had been settled. Then, as further evidence, he added: "One time I had a little spicky in this class. I thought, 'There goes my theory.' But then," he said, as his eyes lit up, "I realized that spics are from Spain, and that's Europe." My sister and I couldn't believe that a Hispanic had actually lived up here, but we felt sorry for whomever it was.

While Alexandra suffered through summer school, I was sent to the local Boy Scout camp. Since I didn't belong to a local troop, I was always assigned to the hodgepodge unit for unaffiliated campers. We learned to tie knots and lash together poles, swam, and practiced CPR. I had by then cultivated a love of credentials and earned as many merit badges as I could each summer. I had collected enough to make the rank of Eagle Scout but, with no scoutmaster in New York or anywhere else, had no one to confer the title upon me.

This particular summer I was assigned to a troop of mentally disabled kids and, much to my surprise, had a great time with them. The disabled kids were entirely unselfconscious; we sat around each other's tents, talking and farting. They did not laugh or sneer at each other's gas, but would break wind in the middle of a sentence and continue unperturbed. No one snapped on anyone else, and I could feel tension fall off my shoulders like molted skin.

All was well until Sunday rolled around. After morning formation, the scoutmaster announced that we would be hiking to a local church. I panicked. I had never been to church before, and I figured that once there I would have to do things I didn't know how to do—like pray. I needed to escape. At the age of ten I had already developed a streak of Jewish self-loathing. With my Irish last name I passed just fine, and I had no desire to admit my ethnicity to anyone in rural Pennsylvania—even the disabled kids in my troop, who surely did not harbor any racial or ethnic prejudices. But in this instance I figured it came down to a choice between admitting my Semitic origins and being exposed in church when I didn't pray correctly.

Suddenly I was angry with my parents for not having properly introduced me to this world of the spirit. In particular, I couldn't understand why my father never explained anything about his religious background to me, information that would have come in handy that Sunday morning. Anytime I had asked my father what he was in terms of religious identity, he merely answered: "I believe in the Giants and the *Form*." We even used to call his *Racing Form* "the Bible," since he pored over it like a scholar studying a sacred text. When I pressed him he admitted that he was Lutheran, though he would not or could not elaborate on what this meant. His own father had hated organized religion, as had his father before him. Steve took particular relish in telling how his paternal grandfather had told a priest to go to hell after the church forbade him from burying his wife, who had died during childbirth, with the stillborn infant, since the latter had not been baptized. He immediately converted to the Lutheran faith of his late Dutch wife and passed this religion on to the surviving members of the next generation.

I had no choice but to opt out of the trek to the local church. Instead of telling the scoutmaster himself, I approached his assistant, who had a beard and long hair and often wore a tie-dyed shirt. I had never known anyone who dressed like him, though I had seen such individuals at the anti-nuclear rally I had attended. Somehow I had internalized a cultural vocabulary that told me that his attire meant he would be more understanding of my religious inexperience than the neatly pressed head scoutmaster would.

"Excuse me," I said to him, as he was busy teasing out the snarls in his red beard with the comb from his Swiss army knife. "I can't go to church today."

"God doesn't care how you look, as long as you show up," he said, a smile detectable underneath his furry visage.

"But I'm—I'm not Catholic," I stuttered.

"That's all right," he answered swiftly and with a knowing glance that implied empathy. "This is a Methodist church."

I didn't think he understood my statement, so I repeated it. He, in turn, reiterated the denomination of the church we would be attending. I had no idea what Methodist meant, but I clued in to the fact that I had made some grave error in my use of terms. Only after I got home from camp did I find out I had conflated Catholicism in particular with Christianity in general. As a result of this misstatement, I had to march down the dirt road to the Methodist church with the rest of the disabled troop. I stood when everyone else stood, sat when they sat, mumbled along during the prayers, said "amen" occasionally, and tried to stay awake when the preacher spoke at length. There was nothing to it. Marching home, I felt I had learned an important new skill that should have earned a merit badge. In that moment, freshly blessed in my Boy Scout fatigues, I felt more like an American than ever before.

After returning from Pennsylvania that year, I started junior high school. The children at Intermediate School 70—the O. Henry School—were a mix of all races and classes. They included the privileged kids from P.S. 41, who now trekked one neighborhood northward, along with black and Hispanic students from the West Side projects and those of us who bused in from other parts of the city. Given how integrated it was, this school seemingly had the potential to sew the two halves of my life together. Little did I realize that putting many races in the same school did not necessarily result in integration. Academic tracking reproduced, to some extent, the larger society's hierarchy of race and class. Moreover, those of us who were poor sat inside, eating our federally subsidized hot lunches, while the Village kids went out to the local shops for food. These institutional forces only abetted the natural tendency of preteens to fall into cliques. And at I.S. 70, *clique* was short for race-class grouping.

There was no school bus for junior high; those of us coming from far away took public transportation. My neighbors and I took the M14 bus, riding from one end of the line to the other. The irony was that I.S. 70 was as rough as the schools in my own neighborhood, largely because it sat next to Charles Evans Hughes High School, a remedial facility for dropouts and students with behavioral problems. Consequently, the I.S. 70 cliques fell into two overall groups: those who became apprentices of the Hughes hoodlums, and those who became their victims. At one point during my tenure there, a teacher was stabbed in the back when he tried to break up a fight between two twelve-year-olds. His name, ironically, was Mr. Sward—pronounced like the weapon.

With a few notable exceptions—Mr. Sward included—the teachers were as tough and merciless as the student body. They ran the school like a prison. We were locked inside the building for the entire day, except at lunch. Even with the school sealed off from the outer world, many teachers forbade students from exiting their rooms once the bell rang. The most drastic restraint of all was imposed in the cafeteria, which was closed off during each lunch period and left under the command of the thick-browed science teacher, Mr. Baumann. He stood against the green-tiled wall with a heavy microphone that transmitted his voice to every corner of the huge room. He used this microphone for more than just talking, however.

"Yo," he yelled at me one day when I was flinging mashed sweet potatoes at my new friend Marcus. "You in the blue shirt, come 'ere. And you, too," he added, pointing to Marcus. Marcus was black and lived in Harlem. He didn't fit in any particular clique, since hardly any other students commuted from his faraway neighborhood. Marcus was the only person who ever referred to me as "nigga." Every time he applied the word to me I relished the sound of it, as I might savor an exotic delicacy. This word, more than any other cultural term or practice, continued to separate me from my neighbors back home. They all referred to each other by this term, whereas I substituted the word *man*, as in, "Yo, what's up, man?" Several times the n-word perched on the edge of my tongue like a diver, ready to leap off. I so desperately wanted to say it. Even many light-skinned Puerto Ricans used the term freely. What would happen if I just casually slipped it in there once? I wondered, playing out the possible scenarios in my head. The more I thought about it, the more I convinced myself that the ability to utter the word *nigga* was the ultimate gulf between my neighbors and me. Even with Marcus I had never uttered the word.

When Mr. Baumann singled Marcus and me out, we had no choice but to stand against the wall with the other students who had erred in some way. We were to spend the rest of our lunch period standing there silently. But Marcus suffered an additional punishment—Mr. Baumann rapped him over the head with the microphone when we arrived at the front of the lunchroom. He conked many kids on the skull with his instrument of oration, leaving a trail of bumps that even the most inexperienced phrenologist could read. What the bumps spelled out was racism; for he never struck me or Michael Holt or even the Turkish Ozan Gurel across our still-hardening cranial plates. He only beaned the black and Hispanic kids.

Afros had gone out of fashion, replaced by close-cropped

hairstyles that left black students with little natural protection from Mr. Baumann's blows. After Marcus was attacked, he and I were made to stand for the rest of the period, the bump on his head swelling with each passing minute. This event propelled Michael into his latest and greatest political crusade: to get Mr. Baumann disciplined.

"We will stand up to him," he told Marcus, whose tears had by then dried, leaving dirty streaks down his face. I remember being surprised at Michael's use of "we," since he had never been hit over the head or even made to stand up along the wall. The issue of race never came up when Michael convinced Marcus to go with him to talk to Principal Witty, but the campaign succeeded: Mr. Baumann was taken off the lunchroom detail, and the bruisings stopped. However, as far as I know he was never disciplined for his actions.

I tried my best to avoid the violence of the school, be it from teachers or fellow students, but I did get into a couple fights of my own making. The first was with none other than my buddy Marcus. Sadly, it all started with a joke.

"Two people were in the bathtub when one said to the other, 'Pass the soap,' " a white kid told Marcus and me. "The other said, 'No soap, *radio*.' " Marcus and the other kid roared with laughter. I laughed too, though after they did and in a higher pitch. As soon as I did, the two of them whipped their heads around to me.

"Why are you laughing?" Marcus asked me.

"Because of the joke."

"What joke?" the other kid interjected.

"The joke," I repeated.

"What's so funny about it?" Marcus asked, his fists on his hips.

"There's no joke. Why's it funny?" the other kid said in rapid succession.

I had only laughed because *they* had. But I couldn't admit that to them, so I quickly invented a punch line. "The second person in the bathtub said 'No soap' and was going to pass him the radio instead," I explained.

"Say what?"

"And anyone who uses a radio in the bathtub," I continued, "is going to electrocute themselves, so he's an idiot. And that's why it's funny."

Marcus's face twisted up in disgust as if he had just sucked on a lemon. "What?" he and the white kid uttered in unison.

"Okay," I said, revising my interpretation. "It's funny because you said there were two guys in the bathtub, so that makes them fags."

"I said two *people*," the white kid instructed, spit flying into my face as he spelled out the word for me. "P-E-O-P-L-E!"

Someone else told me this joke the following week, and I laughed again; when confronted about the source of the hilarity, I changed my strategy. "Come on, you know," I said, giving the person who had told the joke a conspiratorial elbow nudge. That didn't work either, and they stomped off laughing. I spent days trying to figure out the essence of the joke. I looked up each word in the dictionary—*soap*, *radio*, even *no*—

trying to determine if there were multiple meanings that could generate the humor. I finally designed an experiment to figure it out once and for all: I told the joke to my sister. After the punch line, she stood there silently. I observed her as if I were dressed in a white lab coat and holding a stopwatch. "Why aren't you laughing?" I asked finally.

"Because that's the oldest joke in the book," she said. "Don't tell me you laughed at it?"

"No, I—"

"You're not supposed to laugh," she explained in a sympathetic tone. "That's the joke; everybody who knows not to laugh laughs at the person who does."

I became obsessed with this fundamentally different type of dis. *No soap radio* seemed to embody the spirit of junior high school. It was all about centers and peripheries, conformity and deviance, in-groups and out-groups. Since cliques generally fell along race and class lines, I felt particularly stung by Marcus's alliance with the white kid from Greenwich Village.

I had by then come to the realization that the *your momma* snaps so popular in my neighborhood were not really intended to hurt me or the person against whom they were directed; on the contrary, they served to bring everyone together. If someone said my mother was so stupid that she tried to alphabetize M&Ms or that I was so poor that I lived on Avenue E, the imaginary street that would have lain the next block over from Avenue D, I laughed along with everyone else and even gave high fives for particularly good snaps. I got into the rhythm, shouting back that *his* mother was like the library: open to the public. The *no soap radio* joke was different. It was not direct and up front with its humor, not sporting; it was instead about ganging up on someone behind his back, making a person look stupid rather than calling him so.

I carefully planned how I would react the next time this joke was told in front of me. I rehearsed acting blasé, saying "Ha, ha," in a deadpan voice, even adding "How droll" for sarcasm. Finally, a month later, I got my chance. Marcus told the joke to someone during drama class, which was held backstage of the main auditorium. It was May already, and the air was dripping with humidity and with anticipation of summer vacation. The space was dusty and smelled of mildew and antiques, an odor more appropriate for a condemned Broadway theater than a junior high school. Sealed off from the rest of the world, the room functioned as a self-contained ecosystem, the air thick and sticky, like a muddy fog.

I was sitting next to Marcus, waiting for the tardy teacher to show up. Both of us were sucking on red lollipops we had bought during our lunch hour. The dank air coated our lollipops as we waved them through the air to punctuate our snaps on each other. "Your momma's so ugly," Marcus said as he jabbed the air in front of my face with his sucker, "Bigfoot takes pictures of *her*."

I laughed and volleyed back. "Your momma's so poor, I went to her house and her mat said 'Wel—' "

"Oh yeah, well—," he started to say.

I was on the best roll of my life, rattling off one snap after another off in an unselfconscious rhythm that I had never before possessed. "Your momma's so hairy, she look like she got Buckwheat in a headlock."

Marcus was growing frustrated, sucking his lollipop so hard that his cheeks hollowed out completely, and I could discern the outline of the spherical candy inside. He stuttered, starting to fire back, but instead turned to the white girl who was sitting behind him. "Two guys were in the bathtub—," he started. This was my chance to make him look stupid by not laughing, but I couldn't contain my energy or the anger left over from the times I had been the butt of the joke. I grabbed Marcus by his t-shirt, ripping it a bit where the elastic neck met the main body of the garment. "Very funny!" I screamed into his shocked face. His lollipop fell out of his mouth, and I tugged at the ripped collar of his t-shirt. We spun each other around as if we were on the teacup ride at an amusement park, pushing through the heavy curtain that separated the classroom area from the stage. The rest of the class followed. We let go of each other, and I exploded in an involuntary fit, my arms flailing against Marcus's face. One of these epileptic punches landed on his jaw, stunning him for a moment. He quickly recovered, however, and threw a hook that caught the tip of my nose. Blood flowed down and off my face. A cheer erupted from the rest of the class. I punched back, cracking Marcus's close-shaven head with the white of my knuckles. Then I landed a straight punch that smushed his flat nose even flatter into his face. His blood flowed, too, cascading over his lips and onto his shirt.

I felt myself gaining control of the situation as I pummeled

Marcus, who collapsed in a pile of limbs. The class was roaring, and I started crying, not for myself but for Marcus. Some white kids came up to me, slapping me on the back in congratulation. I was still bawling when I bent over to look at Marcus, who had not shed a tear and remained stoic while lying crumpled on the dusty floor. I reached out to try and help him up just as the teacher entered on the scene. When she saw me standing there covered in blood, my hand extended, she yanked me by the ear and took me to the assistant principal's office, where I was suspended for the first time. Then sixth grade ended, and Marcus and I never spoke to each other again.

While things may have been getting worse for me socially at I.S. 70, at home our family's economic situation was improving. My mother had sold her first novel, *Soho Madonna*. Her manuscript had floundered for years with the title *Slum Goddess*, but when she moved the setting a few blocks west to the up-and-coming Soho district and made the family upwardly mobile instead of economically stagnant, the manuscript sold. In 1980 it became the first paperback ever reviewed in the *New York Times*, getting a rave.

Shortly after it was released, Alexandra came home from school crying. "Why didn't you put me on the cover instead of Ashley?" she asked my mother, who didn't understand what my sister was talking about.

"What, sweetie?" she asked, stroking Alexandra's hair as she had when the cornrows hadn't worked out a few years earlier.

"You put Ashley on the cover of your book," my sister sobbed. My mother had played no part in the cover design and didn't know who this Ashley was. But after some deciphering, she figured out that Alexandra was upset because one of her classmates had been hired to model for the cover illustration of the Soho mother and her children. Such are the coincidences one may encounter when attending public school in Manhattan.

My sister had tested into a magnet school in Chinatown. After my experience at the Mini School, my parents hadn't even considered sending her there and immediately enrolled her at P.S. 124, the Yung Wing Elementary School. There Alexandra took classes with a mix of whites, Asians, and other minority students. Her classmates included the child star of *Kramer vs. Kramer* and a renowned piano prodigy who spoke five languages. She never seemed to experience the type of angst about bringing richer friends over to our house that I'd suffered with Michael. Her friends—some of whom were being raised on completely macrobiotic diets—loved the pizzas that my mother let us make. One girl who was forbidden to watch television at home invariably stayed up all night enjoying the late shows with my mother. Another, whose parents did not believe in meals and mealtimes but preferred "grazing" instead, used to beg my mother for a couple of slices of white bread to cure her insomnia.

Only once did Alexandra feel the sense of shame that I seemed to experience regularly. One night Bosi, one of the wealthiest girls from her class, slept over. They needed hair clips with artificial feathers to do themselves up in the correct grade-school style of that time, so my mother took them both to a trinket store on Rivington Street. Rivington Street was at that time the main channel of heroin imports into the United

States; something like 80 percent of the nation's supply passed through Rivington Street. A lot of it was consumed right there as well. The street, a block or two from our house, formed one-third of a worldwide drug circuit, the other two points being the Golden Triangle, a poppy-growing region centered in Burma, and Thailand, where the drugs were shipped en route to Rivington Street.

The girls bought the hair implements and were just exiting the store when gunfire erupted. My mother pushed Bosi and my sister face down onto the lugie-ridden pavement. They got back safely, but my sister remained uncharacteristically quiet for the rest of the evening. Bosi never came over again.

That incident aside, Alexandra seemed as confident as I was insecure, as charming as I was awkward. She had birthday parties where practically everyone from her class showed up. Almost everyone wanted a turn to sleep over, and almost everyone got one—except Ashley, who never made the list after appearing on the cover of my mother's novel.

Soho Madonna also caused friction between my sister and her teacher. Each student had received an assignment to bring in a book from home and read a section of it to the entire class. My sister chose our mother's book. The teacher, Ms. Edelson, opened to a random page and instructed Alexandra to start there. She did, reading a section where Jobina, the protagonist, suspected that her artist husband, Mack, was cheating on her: *"There seemed to be no way to check. But what if you could weigh the balls? What if there were some way you could weigh the balls to see if they were empty or full—"*

Alexandra got no further. She didn't get a chance to narrate how Jobina established baseline testicle measurements by flattering Mack on his manliness until he agreed to place his scrotum on her Weight Watchers scale; how she charted the change in their mass after sex; how she confirmed her suspicions with scientific data. After reading three short sentences, Alexandra was yanked from the front of the room, screamed at by Ms. Edelson, and ushered into the principal's office along with the "smut." She was about to be suspended when my mother roared into the office and explained that the "smut" was her own book. *New York Times* review in hand, Ellen declared that if the teacher or the principal ever made Alexandra feel bad about herself or her mother's work again, she would file a complaint with the Board of Education.

Despite excellent press, *Soho Madonna* failed to make us rich. But that didn't stop my parents from celebrating. Ellen bought leather coats for herself and my father. She gave my sister and me each twenty dollars to take to the 69-cent store. Best of all, she took us all on a trip to Colombia. She had enough money to pay for the airfare but not much more, so we packed our suitcases full of food. My sister and I ate in the hotel room in Cartagena, using a heating coil to cook powdered Lipton soups and canned baked beans. Meanwhile, my parents attended the all-you-can-eat buffets at the hotel, filling their pockets with what they could to bring back to us. Since we had packed few clothes, we pretty much wore the t-shirts we got free from the hotel upon our arrival. The sun was so hot that it burned us through the thin layer of cotton. Alexandra and I swooned with heat fatigue and hunger as we pressed our faces up to the glass of the air-conditioned hotel dining room, watching my father help himself to his third omelet of the morning as the serving girls giggled.

In another effort to save money, my mother opted for an out-of-date copy of Fodor's guide to Colombia. For the most part it worked just fine. But once, while trying to get to a restaurant listed in the guide, we found ourselves waved off in frantic pantomime by the locals. The restaurant was long defunct, replaced by a booby-trapped coca-leaf field in the decade or so since the publication of the guidebook. These incidents notwithstanding, we had a great trip. It was the first time my sister and I had traveled outside the United States. It was the first time I saw real mountains; the ridges of the Andes seemed to slope downward as steeply and jaggedly as the price chart for a crashing stock market, right to the edge of the sea and almost into it, as if they were marching into the ocean peak by peak.

We were also fascinated and disturbed by the local poverty. The Colombian villagers seemed to endure a material hardship much harsher than anything we had witnessed in New York City; only the homeless veterans who begged on the subway, those with oozing sores or missing limbs, seemed to offer a comparison. The sight of Colombian children with flies eating at their eyes and blind old ladies who seemed to shrivel up right before us brought waves of sickness to my stomach. I kept telling myself that at least it was warm here, at least they didn't have to worry about freezing to death as some of the

New York homeless did. It didn't help, though. I still felt as if a hole were being eaten in the lining of my stomach. I rushed past, trying not to look, imagining that I had on blinders like some of the horses back at Aqueduct.

The biggest shock of all, however, was the prevalence of guns. While we knew there were guns back home, we almost never saw one. When a gun was shown—as when Bosi and my sister had hit the pavement on Rivington Street or when a robber took hostages at the local drugstore—it was invariably used. In this respect, life on the Lower East Side seemed to follow the rules of stage drama. In Colombia, by contrast, huge machine guns were everywhere. Government officers in military garb wore them on their shoulders, with spare rounds of ammo hung around their necks like leis. The soldiers' fingers sat on the triggers, and my sister and I could not escape the feeling that gunfire was always imminent. But the threat of violence came from the state, not from the people themselves. The Colombians seemed so calm and peaceful that I had trouble imagining what would actually provoke the soldiers to fire their weapons. We had heard stories of bandits in the mountains, but the locals we encountered seemed to be the most docile folks on earth. At the time it didn't occur to me that perhaps this was a matter of cause and effect, that the submissiveness of the villagers might be a coping mechanism, the result of years of state oppression.

Our short burst of luxurious living at the equator heralded a general improvement in our financial situation. My father, who only occasionally sold a piece of work despite rave reviews from Tom Wolfe, among others, now took a part-time job to support the family. Initially he served as a messenger for *Time* magazine, hand-delivering the final page proofs from the headquarters in New York to the printing plant in Chicago. He got to spend one night a week living large on a corporate account and always brought my sister and me some airline peanuts or a set of toy captain's wings. My mother couldn't be assuaged so easily, however, and resented his weekly escape from us. Soon this boondoggle ended, and he was offered a job in the New York office for two long days a week, pasting up page layouts. It always took him a third day to recover from the double shift and the harsh chemical solvents involved in the work, and he began to complain that he had no time for his art, given his share of the child care and housework responsibilities. He never gave up the weekly trip to the racetrack, however. When his job ratcheted up to three days of long hours and his mother was diagnosed with cancer, my father's free time disappeared altogether. He never got the chance to capitalize on his critical acclaim in the art world and began to fall into an alcohol-aided depression, which worsened when his mother died. It took him a year or two to work through the grieving process, but he continued to resent his day job until the day he retired over twenty years later.

Looking back, I believe my father's attitude toward work marked our class position more than any other psychological dynamic within the family. While other men in the neighborhood might have felt down on themselves for not having a job or not getting enough hours of work, my father had the opposite reaction. As long as he had been a full-time artist who got by on odd jobs, he was someone special, someone whose position in life could not be captured by his income or occupation. But as soon as he slipped into regular work at a regular job, he ceased to feel like an artist, one who existed outside the socioeconomic structures of American society. He had become what he despised, a workingman. Now he was simply lower middle class—and downwardly mobile from his corporate-class father to boot. There was no escaping it or denying it, and he didn't try to. It was the single biggest sacrifice he made for the family, one he sustained for twenty years and for which he received little in the way of thanks.

My sister and I may not have appreciated the economic transformation we were going through at the time, but we did notice that some things changed when my father started working. They were not related to the extra income we enjoyed as a family but rather to the in-kind payment that accompanied it. Suddenly we had an unlimited supply of pens, pencils, and paper. When I had to take drafting class at school, my father got me a protractor, a professional compass, and a couple of other instruments—all for free, courtesy of Time, Inc. No more did we scrounge for half-used pens and pencils on the floor at school or use the backsides of junk mail instead of notebooks. I felt proud to open my knapsack at school, particularly since everything had *Time* written all over it. And T-I-M-E spelled respectability.

I had lost Marcus through my own belligerence. I had also drifted apart from Michael almost from the day we started at the new school; the following year he was accepted into Hunter, one of the best public schools in the city, and left I.S. 70. Luckily, that semester I made a new friend. Jerome McGill was black and commuted from my neighborhood. The first year we never seemed to take the same bus to school, but during seventh grade we got to know each other during our daily ride on the M14. Looking back, it seems eerie that I became friends with Jerome not too long after I had my fight with Marcus. It was almost as if I had a certain slot in my life for a black friend, which could be filled by only one individual at a time—although I hope this was not the case, that it was merely a coincidence.

Jerome lived a couple of blocks up on Avenue D, in a housing complex that was even more dangerous and much more hopeless than ours. Few of the residents there worked at all. Jerome smiled a lot. He smiled despite the fact that he'd lost his dad early in his childhood. His father had been sunning himself in a plastic lounge chair on the fire escape when one leg of the foldout chaise got caught and tipped him over and off as he tried to stand up. Jerome kept smiling even though his mother worked all the time, even though he had to take care of his younger sister Zuni, who was Alexandra's age, when he would rather have played stickball or stoop with the rest of us, even though he had little money to spend on Reggie Bars or Mike and Ike candies. In fact, Jerome never stopped smiling.

He had straight white teeth with a slight overbite. He was tall for his age but slim to the point of looking slightly malnourished. His elbows protruded as if the bones were growing so fast that the skin could not keep up. His bearing stood out from the typical countenance in the neighborhood. Most people walked with their shoulders stooped and their heads down, as if nothing going on around them was interesting enough to elicit their attention. Jerome, by contrast, always walked as if he had somewhere to be, his head up, chin out, his long limbs springing ahead as if they knew themselves where that somewhere was. As he glided through the projects or down Avenue D, he made eye contact with passersby. This, too, set him apart from the rest of us, especially from me. On the West Side I stared down every man, woman, or child who crossed my path, but back in the neighborhood I looked down or out of the corner of my eye. Eye contact on Avenue D meant confrontation, and confrontation meant the potential for violence, which I would be sure to receive rather than dole out. Jerome's gaze had quite the opposite effect, disarming everyone in his path. He nodded to old ladies and aggressive teenagers alike, as if he were the very glue that held the community together.

He certainly was the singular drop of Krazy Glue that kept me connected to other kids after my tenure on Las Piratas had ended. Often he coaxed me past the steel bars and down the twenty-one flights of stairs to hang out on the benches with the neighborhood kids, even Sean. One time, not too long after we had met, we were hanging out after school near his house with some of the ex-Piratas when someone suggested bus riding—that is, hopping onto the back of the M14 and riding it like an urban bucking bronco. The trick was to jump onto the back bumper just as the bus turned off Avenue D and headed toward the river before swinging around the projects to come back down Delancey Street, ready for another journey northward and westward. There were seldom any passengers on this final portion of the route; with no additional weight and no stops, the bus driver could really take off, whipping around the FDR Drive at speeds that must have come close to the vehicle's maximum. The velocity, the sharp turns, and the fact that the bus came back around almost to the starting point made this stretch the favorite among bus jockeys.

Clinton, the catcher for Las Piratas, grabbed hold of a ridge of the corrugated metal that armored the outside of the bus and was whisked away on his plastic banana-shaped skateboard. At the same time, Sean hopped the bumper and grasped the ridge of the Gloria Vanderbilt blue jeans advertisement that was plastered on the back of the bus. As the bus sped off he waved to Jerome and me, humping the picture of a woman's buttocks tightly clad in the designer jeans.

Jerome and I were supposed to take the next bus, which was following close behind. But my mother had made me swear not to ride the back of the buses. She had, as was her way, even bribed me with a cash payment. In exchange for two dollars and a trip to the 69-cent store, I had signed an affidavit stating that I would never "ride on the outside of any bus or other motor vehicle in any manner or fashion, alone or in combination with a skateboard, bicycle or other motor or non-motor vehicle." Though only ten at the time, I had already negotiated many such contracts with my mother. For sums ranging from a quarter to five dollars I had forsaken my right to lean over the subway platform to check if the train was coming, to haggle with a mugger, even to commit suicide. That last one had earned me a full five-dollar note. It was easy money, since suicide was a concept that was then well beyond my grasp, let alone my desire. But I'd once threatened to kill myself if she didn't let me go over to the next project with some of the Piratas.

"Don't ever say that!" my mother had scolded, in a tone harsher than I had ever heard her use. Without even stopping to explain, she cupped her hand over my mouth and nose and held it there for what seemed like several minutes but must have been only thirty or forty seconds. "You want to know what death tastes like?" she asked, pressing the back of my head into her other palm as I struggled for air. "This is a little bit of death. This is what it's like."

Unlike my father, she never struck us, so this was the most

violent she had ever been with me. When she removed her hand, air rushed into me seemingly beyond my control. My head was spinning, as much from seeing a mother I didn't recognize as from lack of oxygen. Finally, as the color came back to both our faces, the mother I knew returned. "Promise me that you will never kill yourself," she said as softly as she stroked my hair. Later that day she left out a contract for me to sign. There was none of the negotiation that usually went on between us, and at bedtime I found a five-dollar bill stuck under my pillow. Nothing else was ever said.

As for my agreement to ride only on the inside of buses, that was another story. She had repeated her warning—or, rather, her legal dictum—every so often when she saw another kid doing it. Earlier that week she had waved the contract, or something that looked like it, in front of me as she recited its contents by heart. I don't know if she could sense something in the works or if, perhaps, her warning actually planted the suggestion in my head, but for whatever reason I found myself standing on the corner with Jerome, poised to hop the next bus, which sat waiting for the light to change. It certainly had not been my idea, so I could not discount the possibility of maternal ESP.

"Ready?" Jerome asked as the light changed to green. He saw the hesitancy in my step and immediately came to a halt himself. "You can't?" he asked. I nodded. I braced myself for a lecture on how not to be scared. Instead, Jerome's own ESP kicked in.

"Your mother?"

I nodded again. Jerome had spent enough time in our house to know how things worked in our family. Without saying anything else, he started walking toward the East River. I followed silently as we circled the Baruch houses, trailing the black stream of smoke left in the wake of the bus. Just as we rounded the block and were coming up Delancey Street, he started running. I ran, too. As breathless as when my mother had cupped her hand over my mouth and nose, I followed him to the corner where Sean and Clinton stood.

"Yo, what happened?" Sean asked.

I looked down, ashamed of having copped out, but Jerome spoke up. "Yo," he said. "We got busted."

"Word?" Clinton asked.

"Yeah," Jerome continued. "The driver was going to have us arrested. That's why we had to run here." I had never seen Jerome lie to anyone before. No one seemed to notice the fact that the bus had pulled in too far ahead of us to make our story believable.

Just as he saved what little face I had that afternoon, Jerome brought my sister into the male fold. Whenever we played touch football or whiffle ball in the playground area of the project, he would pick my sister for his team. The other kids would grumble about it, and I would wince and blush, my entire face turning as red as my lips. But Jerome would override any resentments with his huge smile and a wink.

Not only did Jerome repair my ties with Sean and the other neighborhood kids, he was also my best friend at school. I remember one particular afternoon late in seventh grade when a schoolwide assembly was convened in the auditorium to select the music for an end-of-year party. Most of the black and Hispanic kids liked disco, while the white kids from the Village liked rock, punk, or new wave. When word got around that the selection of music was the purpose of the assembly, the student body segregated into camps that were scaled-down versions of the neighborhoods from which we came. All the black and Hispanic kids sat on the left side of the room, while the whites sat on the right. Lacking any strong musical opinions—I only knew I liked my father's reggae over my mother's country and western—I had no idea where to sit. I thought I would literally be left standing in the aisle that divided disco from rock. I saw Marcus sitting on the disco side, chatting with some friends. There was a seat free next to him, but when he made eye contact with me my stomach rose up into my throat and my heart dropped into the space my stomach had occupied. We had not spoken since our fight the year before. I was about to leave the auditorium altogether and pass the period sitting in the stall of one of the bathrooms when Jerome called out, smiled, and patted the seat next to him, beckoning me to join him on the disco side.

I sat down next to him and craned my neck, searching the other side of the aisle for Ozan or some of the other kids I knew. But the white kids were the bigger group, and there were too many pale faces and too many shaggy mops of hair obscuring facial features. Seeing the races separated out this way, it struck me just how different the two groups at I.S. 70 were from one another. The white kids, like their hairdos, were all carefully disheveled in style. Their Levi's gathered at the crotch and bunched into folds at the ankle where they met their shoes. They wore loose-fitting t-shirts that hung out over their pants. The shirts either were a solid color or advertised a recent rock concert by the Who, Foreigner, or Boston. Some wore denim jackets despite the mid-spring warmth; others had on headbands, barrettes, or hair clips, though few wore any sort of hat. The punks sported ripped t-shirts and pierced various parts of their faces with safety pins. Their hair was gelled up into spikes or shaved into Mohawks. By contrast, the headbangers had the longest, most tangled hair of all, completely obscuring their faces.

These two subcultures were minorities among the white majority, whose biggest musical preference was so-called classic rock. It had been about a decade since the breakup of the Beatles and the deaths of Jim Morrison, Jimi Hendrix, and Janis Joplin, but already the music of the Sixties and early Seventies had been canonized. It was as if the world had started at the time of our births and history had been compressed to fit our short life spans. Nostalgia was the reigning ethos among the Village kids; the world as they knew it seemingly had peaked by 1970.

The darker side of the aisle shared none of this cultural longing for the past. The Sugar Hill Gang had recently released "Rapper's Delight," the commercial precursor to hip hop, and public space back home seemed to spill over with musical artifacts thanks to the advent of boom boxes and the nonexistence of Walkmans. Proto–break dancing had emerged in the playground and on the streets. Exciting new sneaker and clothing brands seemed to pop up daily for our consumer pleasure. We were on the cusp of cultural renaissance. The theme of dress was tight, striped, and labeled. T-shirts hugged the well-defined pubescent musculature of the boys and the developing breasts of the girls. Girls wore designer jeans that hugged nascent hips, with stripes down the sides tracing their paths of development. Shorts also had stripes down the sides of them, often matching those on the accompanying shirts. Even tube socks, pulled up tight so that they almost reached the knee, proudly displayed three horizontal stripes across the top end—the thicker the better. And on our side of the aisle, designer labels served as status markers. A lot of the minority girls wore Gloria Vanderbilt or Sergio Valente jeans, while the boys had the trademarks of their favorite sneaker brands, such as Converse or Adidas, splashed across their chests. Others wore the same Izod Lacoste golf shirts that my grandparents donned on the links.

Sitting among this group, I felt disheveled with the exception of my pseudo-Izod shirt, which I had constructed that summer by sewing a stolen alligator over the Sears logo. I had swiped the Izod badge from my grandparents' house, where I would sneak into the bedroom and rummage through the clothing drawers in search of designer labels. All the clothes I wore—right down to my underwear—were inherited from a boy a couple years older than me whose family lived next door to my grandparents. My mother used to joke that if the police ever found me unconscious after an accident they would probably call the wrong family, since everything I wore had the name Jeff Frey sewn into it. Most of this hand-me-down clothing came from Sears. I'd have preferred those clothes without their logos, but Sears sewed its emblem into all its clothing. Instead of an Izod alligator on my breast, I had a dragon. Instead of a little red or orange Levi's tag on the back pocket of my pants, I had a large brown plastic Toughskins label. My solution to this problem was simple: I replaced the labels I didn't like with better ones, trading up from Sears to John Weitz or Izod if I could find the right insignia on my grandparents' clothes. At first I only took tags that appeared to be loose or whose absence wouldn't be noticed right away. But eventually I took to ripping intact labels clear off their original garments so I could graft them onto my own wardrobe. I was more worried about being discovered wearing doctored designer labels than I was about my skin color being an issue on the disco, minority side of the aisle.

The assembly to select the music for the school party began, and it got rowdy in a hurry. The assistant principal tried to solicit nominations for songs from the audience, but he was soon drowned out by competing chants that had emerged from the crowd. He was the strictest disciplinarian among the administrators, the same official who had suspended me for my fight with Marcus, but he quickly lost control of the proceedings. The white kids started in with the chant "Disco sucks!" It grew louder with each utterance; when our side of the aisle tried to retaliate with "Rock sucks!" it lacked the same ring.

"Okay, okay!" the assistant principal shouted over the loudspeaker. "Let's vote." Everyone quieted down for a moment as he appealed to democracy: "Everyone who wants disco, raise your hand."

Our side of the room lifted its arms. Many of the kids raised two hands, trying to cast a double vote. Some stretched as tall as they could, desperate to be noticed and have their preference counted. Others actually stood up on their chairs, waving their arms in the air. Then the assistant principal asked who wanted rock. Despite the efforts of the minority kids to project a show of force, the white kids won out by their sheer numbers. Though ours was an integrated school, minorities were still just that—minorities, outnumbered by the white kids in the population. When the assistant principal declared on his eyeball count that rock had won, the white kids erupted back into their chant: "Disco sucks, disco sucks!"

Then someone from our side of the aisle defied the schoolwide ban on boom boxes and cranked Queen's "Another One Bites the Dust" to full volume. That song and those on Madonna's first album, which had just been released, were about the only music that crossed the taste lines of race. School security hustled through the milling crowd to find the source of the mega bass; they seized the radio, but it took them a moment or two to find the off switch. In the meantime, a blond kid from the rock side yelled over, "Hey, Queen is white anyway, and they're rock and roll!"

"Queen ain't white!"

"Yeah, they are," someone else from the other group chimed in. "They're even gay."

"Queen ain't no faggots!"

"Mm hmmm," the blond kid replied. The level of tension had risen, and I was sure that a fight would break out at any moment. I wanted to signal that I was on the disco side despite my light skin, since I was fairly confident that if it came to fisticuffs disco would triumph despite its less numerous defenders. This was the macho consolation prize of being oppressed: the reputation for toughness. The possibility of a rumble felt different from the potential one-on-one confrontations in which I had been involved. I was much less nervous now than I had been when tangling with James for my glove or being held hostage by Sean. Being part of an army of sorts felt protective in a way, even if the reality was that a rumble broke down to hand-to-hand combat. I guess I assumed that if I were in trouble in a rumble someone on my side would help me out, because the strength and honor of the entire group would be at stake.

I turned to Jerome for answers. Like most people on my side of the aisle, I had always assumed that Queen was black. Jerome shrugged his shoulders. Then someone else from our group yelled, "He's right. Queen is white; they're from England." The boy hung his head as he said this, as if he were admitting some horrible atrocity that his people had committed. He was a ninth-grader and thus had authority, so his words dissipated the primed-up, pugilistic energy of our side like a knife slashing the tires of a sports car. Our confidence gave way to a sense of cultural defeat, an unspoken presumption that the white kids would always be right, even about things we thought belonged to us. Our image of ourselves as makers and beneficiaries of a cultural renaissance disappeared for the time being.

The bell rang for the start of the next period. As we all filed out, people were chanting "Rock and roll will never die!"

We had lost, but all I remember feeling was content. For the first time I felt I could be who I wanted to be—albeit with Jerome's help. At the time I didn't realize that Jerome was more than just an aid in this process; he was the essential catalyst, without whom I would have been just as lost as I had been ever since my Mini School days. Only after I had lost Jerome from my life would I fully realize what he meant to me.

Over the course of seventh grade, Jerome and I spent more and more time together, alternating between playing video games at the Twin Donut near I.S. 70 and trying to invent our own by programming computers at the Radio Shack on Broadway. The owner of the electronics franchise, which was situated about halfway between school and home, thought it made good publicity to have kids sitting in the store window clacking away at the keys of his floor models. Several of us from Avenue D spent our after-school hours there, writing our own versions of Pong or an interactive, computerized version of Dungeons and Dragons.

Now Jerome slept over every Thursday night, and we could hang out as often as we liked, since he only lived a block away—though if our session lasted until after dark my mother made him wait for her to drive him home. Better still, she let him sleep over on nights other than Thursday. We would stay up as late as we could, designing new monsters for whatever version of Dungeons and Dragons we were working on. He drew the characters, and I wrote the accompanying text that explained the powers of whatever half-dragon, half-gnome he had created. I was still an early-morning person, however, and would inevitably fall asleep, drooling on my open book, while Jerome stayed up chatting with my mother as she sipped her Diet Pepsi, discussing whatever self-help gurus she had seen on the talk shows that day.

Our friendship became strong enough that Jerome was the first person with whom I ever jointly bought something. One day after school we pooled our lunch money to buy a sweat-shirt. A man with gray hair and a black goatee had been selling clothes out of the back of a truck parked on the street that sep-arated I.S. 70 from Charles Evans Hughes. The high school stu-dents had already snapped up all the Adidas-brand shorts and t-shirts. Since it was almost summer by then, with tempera-tures over ninety degrees, sweatshirts were going cheap. To-gether, Jerome and I had enough cash to buy one. It was a Champion—soft, fuzzy, and thick, so plush that when I pinched it I couldn't feel my thumb and finger pressing against each other. We were both entranced by what we had pur-chased: quality. It was as if we had discovered the meaning of an abstract concept like good, evil, or God. This was why cer-tain sweatshirts cost more than others, I realized. At the same time, I started to grasp the concept of poverty, as if my adoles-cent logic required every idea to contain within it its dialecti-cal opposite. I felt angry and deprived for never having known what quality was. I also felt defeated in my efforts to catch up with the Village kids. If I saved all my money to make up lost fi-nancial ground, I had to forsake quality in my life. But if I chose to recognize these subtle differences, to cultivate this taste for the good life, which the Village kids took for granted, then I would never better my financial lot.

Though I cursed my predicament, I also was thankful for the opportunity to appreciate something new and better—something like the sweatshirt. I reveled in the notion of upward mobility, joyed by the idea that the present and future generally made for a favorable contrast to the past.

Jerome seemed as astonished as I was by the purchase. He ran his hyperextended palm up and down the garment, first feeling all of the outer knit, then turning it inside out to feel the contrast of the plush interior lining. Then he tugged on the Champion label that was sewn—all four sides—into the collar. It didn't flap off, irritating the neck of the wearer, begging to be torn away. Accompanying this label was a tiny "C" that stuck out of the seam where the body of the shirt met the waistband. I was disappointed to find such a small manifestation of the name brand, upset that the garment didn't have a more prominent declaration of its tony status. But soon I realized I didn't need one. Now I felt silly for all the label sewing I had done over the past two summers and for all the time I'd wasted worrying that someone would check the inside tags of my shirts—a common practice in our school—to see if they matched the insignia on the outside.

When Jerome and I had finished admiring the softness, the thickness, and the ineffable qualities contained within the article of clothing, we made an arrangement to alternate who got to wear it, switching it off each week at the Thursday night sleepover. Soon, however, I sold Jerome my half of "quality" to underwrite a more expensive habit: I had become addicted to video games.

More specifically, I had become addicted to Defender, which I played at the Twin Donut whenever possible. To support my habit I embezzled laundry quarters when I did the weekly wash, skimping on the dryers. I returned the clothes folded but damp, and soon our entire family wardrobe took on the dank smell of mildew. Jerome was just as hooked on the Twin Donut Defender machine as I was, but unlike me he actually improved his performance over time. Before long he could play for more than an hour on a single quarter, while I seemed stuck somewhere at the bottom of the learning curve and had to keep plugging change into the machine.

I sold all my comic books, I sold my Dungeons and Dragons books, and when I ran out of goods to hock I stepped up my illicit activity from embezzlement to naked theft. I stole my sister's savings from her Hello Kitty bank. I took money almost daily from each of my parents. My father kept his racetrack cash in his top drawer, underneath rows of neatly folded socks. He was somewhat careful with his finances, so I had to replace a large-denomination bill with a smaller one so that the overall number of notes and size of the wad remained the same. As long as the same weight and thickness were there, it would take him a while to discover that he was missing five or ten dollars in his total.

Stealing from my mother was easy. Her purse teemed with loose change, a canister of Mace, family photos, and year upon year of receipts. Though Ellen carefully monitored the Diet Pepsi supply, she had no idea how much cash she was holding at any given time. I started by trolling the crevices of her purse, fishing through the crumbled codeine tablets that she swallowed when she had a migraine to locate change and crumpled dollar bills. When I had cleaned out the bottom of her purse, I moved on to her cash compartment. She unfailingly left it unzipped, various bills sticking out like the petals of an origami flower. I plucked them one by one, then two by two.

Soon I was cutting school and convincing Jerome to do the same, bribing him with quarters from my illicit supply. I explained that our records would be cleansed when we moved on to high school anyway, so it didn't matter what marks we earned or what trouble we got ourselves into during these lower grades. All that mattered was the Stuyvesant test, I told him on several occasions. Though I had missed the entrance cutoff for Hunter by a large margin, the next year we were to take an admissions test to a triumvirate of selective high schools: Stuyvesant, Bronx Science, and Brooklyn Tech. Students not lucky enough to get into one of those had to settle for the local public high school or, if they could afford it, Catholic school. The competition was especially tough since many private-school kids took the exam, trying to save their parents thousands of dollars of tuition by getting into an accelerated public high school.

I had managed to avoid having my parents find out about my poor grades by forging my father's already illegible signature on my report card and responding cheerily whenever they asked me how my journalism or history class was going. I never confessed that I had been demoted out of the academic track and placed in the vocational curriculum. These classes were populated predominantly by minority students, a fact to which I failed to ascribe any importance at the time. Journalism had been replaced by sewing, history by typing, and science by wood shop. When I did manage to show up for school, I spent my days crocheting, following patterns, typing make-believe memos, and carving mini totem poles. There were hardly any girls in my classes, despite their home economics flavor. Instead the toughest kids in school, those who were destined for Charles Evans Hughes High School across the street, filled up these classes, which focused on life skills like darning socks, knitting, and changing typewriter ribbons. Little did the educational bureaucrats know that changing typewriter ribbons would be entirely useless in the imminent computer age.

I actually enjoyed school more now that I had given up on it. Being in the lower track gave me a touch of coolness that I had never experienced when I was among the Village kids, reading poetry aloud in English class or running experiments in chemistry lab. Michael, Ozan, and *antidisestablishmentarianism* were ancient history; the two halves of my life, it seemed, were finally being sewn back together.

One incident in particular made me feel as though I were once again part of the community. One day when I had timed my return from Twin Donut to coincide with the end of school, I passed *Sesame Street* Sean sitting with some friends on the back of one of the splintered green benches. He and the other Outlaws had been cultivating their own, more costly addictions that academic year, spending more and more time on the benches with a green or brown bottle dangled between their legs, giving a chill to their thighs in between swigs. When I passed Sean, I looked down and gripped the straps of my book bag with both hands as if I were climbing a mountain and it were my safety harness. Even though I had spent some time with him since the knife incident, Jerome had always been there, too. I felt the floor of my stomach open like a trapdoor when Sean hopped off the back of his bench and followed me from a few steps behind.

"Yo! Yo! My man," the others yelled out to him, not quite in unison. "Where you going, nigga?"

Out of the corner of my eye, I saw Sean waving them off with a backhand motion. My heart leaped over a beat or two, and I felt my legs twitch underneath me. The rest of the malt liquor drinkers on the benches cackled and gave each other high fives when they made the connection that Sean was following me. "He going to get hisself some honky money!" one of them announced, confirming my suspicion. I could feel bile creeping up into my throat.

We turned the corner, becoming invisible to the group. I braced myself, flexing each muscle in my body as I continued my stride, now walking more like a robot than a boy of eleven, thinking the whole time: Do I still have my mugging money? Down came Sean's hand on my shoulder. "Yo, chill out," he said. Sean removed his hand and wiped his nose with the back of it. He was trying to say something but only stuttered and tapped the tip of one sneaker with the heel of the other. Finally he got it out. "I heard you real good at D&D," he said, using the acronym for the role-playing game I had since given up. "Jerome said you could teach me how to play?"

When I finally turned and looked at Sean face-on, he seemed to have shrunk in size; either his verbal vulnerability had shattered his Oz-like illusion of power, or I was catching up to him after his early growth spurt. At any rate, I smiled and muttered "sure" several times before scurrying upstairs.

Sean never pursued the D&D possibility again, and I was too shy to bring it up. But whenever I look back on that encounter, I am touched by his earnestness, by the fact that he asked to play a child's game of die-rolling and storytelling while his fingers gripped an adult's bottle of malt liquor. Dungeons and Dragons was a game of violence, but the killing was imaginary; we could start over when we made a mistake, a luxury we lacked in real life. Fantasy games and violent video games were very popular among the kids in my neighborhood and could have served as a way for me to bond with my peers. I liked Dungeons and Dragons in particular since all the action took place in the mind; although the game involved fighting and killing, it required no physical skills whatsoever, only verbal and written ones. While violent fantasy games may be frowned upon in middle-class suburbs, they may have some therapeutic value in areas where real-life violence is not uncommon to children. I'm sorry I never took Sean up on his request.

At the same time that Jerome was doing his best to reintegrate me into the neighborhood, I was dragging him down the vocational track with me by repeatedly convincing him to cut classes, promising that after we had scored 100,000 points on Defender we would go to the library or Barnes and Noble and read things that would be more educational than sewing class anyway. In reality we only made it to the bookstore once, and that time we read the updated Dungeons and Dragons monster manual.

My video game career ended when my mother caught me. I was having one of my best Defender games ever, setting off dozens of smart bombs while slicing down mutants of all types with my high-tech laser guns. Then my mother dropped the biggest smart bomb of all. She marched into Twin Donut and grabbed me by the ear, just as she had that day after manhunt. Jerome watched, aghast, as did all the Village kids, who were busy buying their morning coffee and cigarettes.

"Hello, Ellen," Jerome said to alert me to my mother's presence, elbowing me at the same time. I couldn't turn around, since I was engaged in a fight with several high-speed attackers over very mountainous terrain. Within two seconds, however, I was being dragged off by the earlobe. "Go to school, Jerome," my mother said in a tone that I had never heard her use with anyone other than my sister or myself. To me she said nothing.

I caught the eye of a blond, shaggy-haired kid who was packing his newly purchased Marlboros, banging the cellophane-covered box against the flesh of his wrist. He wore a white concert t-shirt with black sleeves that stopped halfway up his forearms. My eyes pleaded to his for understanding, begging for sympathy and for merciful restraint when he inevitably reported this incident to others back at school. At first his pale blue eyes seemed to offer such an assurance, but our connection had the half-life of a subatomic particle that exists for only a split second and only under artificial conditions. His eyes became vacant and distant, making it all the more certain that he would relish recounting the scene. He had a choice and opted for the path that most twelve-year-olds would take.

A female classmate had also witnessed the scene as she sipped a hot beverage that was probably more milk and sugar than actual coffee. Her long black hair was always pulled back into a ponytail, individual hairs popping out here and there with the bent stiffness of loose wires in a bundle of cables. This girl had rich parents and was even rich herself, having appeared in a Dr. Pepper commercial. To top it all off, she had already developed breasts and hips, making her one of the most popular girls in the school. When I played the incident over in my head, I realized I had given the shaggy blond boy his chance, his bonding fodder, so that he could make his move on the Dr. Pepper girl.

Never letting go of my ear, my mother pulled me into the Oldsmobile, which sat parked illegally in the bus stop in front of the shop, idling with the door open. I said nothing as we sped off. My mother was driving fast, which was quite unusual for her, and not saying anything, which was almost unheard of. She was so angry she actually ran a red light on Seventh Avenue. We headed east, away from school. I wondered why she had told Jerome to go to school while we were going somewhere else. The whites of her knuckles shone through her skin as she gripped the steering wheel. After a few minutes I realized I had left my knapsack behind in the rush of my forced exit. I told my mother, who still didn't say anything but merely turned around with a great looping U-turn, the car coming about like a huge galleon on Fourteenth Street. But by the time we got back to Twin Donut a quarter of an hour later, the bag was gone, lost to the city's speedy pirates. Only when I had returned to the car empty-handed did she say anything.

"Why?" she asked.

"Why what?" I asked meekly. The words themselves formed a snotty retort, but the tone made all the difference. I really did want to clarify the question. *Why?* took me by surprise. I might have expected *how?* or *when?* or *what?*—getting the facts straight, determining exactly what I had done. By asking *why*, she implied that she already knew everything I had been doing—the stealing, the forgery, the cutting school.

"Why did you lie to me?"

"I didn't lie," I answered, happy that I could give a legalistic, technical answer to the question. I had never actually been asked anything that required a dishonest answer, so I truly hadn't fibbed. Not that I wouldn't have had it been necessary.

"I don't care if you fail out of school," she said. "I don't care if you never graduate from wood shop"—her choice of classes confirmed that she did, in fact, know everything—"I don't care if you never go to school again," she said. "But you must tell the truth."

My mind flashed back to the still unconfessed-to comic-book theft. "I'll study a lot," I offered. "I'll make up all the work. I promise." She didn't respond. "How much do I have to pay?" I asked, resorting to our moral balance of trade. She still said nothing, making me squirm in my seat. Desperate for some sort of response, some resolution, I finally shot out: "None of it matters anyway. As soon as I go to high school, I start with a fresh record. Everything before doesn't count."

She turned to me, shaking. I didn't know whether she would cry or strike me. She did neither. When we got home, she put me in my room and shut the door. I didn't come out until the next day, when I went straight to school without a word to anyone in the house.

The first morning back to school in 1982 did not feel much different than any other. As I waited for the M14 bus, I looked for some sign, something in the air that would indicate or at least imply that it had actually happened—that Jerome had been critically wounded a few days before, only a few blocks from where I boarded the bus every day. Everything was crisp. The unseasonably warm weather that had accompanied the Christmas break had disappeared, and the sky was a uniform dark blue, an almost-faux color that belied the coldness of the air. The roofs of the project apartments formed neat ruler-like lines slicing into the sky. Nothing disrupted the stillness except a flock of pet pigeons, which formed black ink dots across the blue background as they circled above the Avenue D tenements.

I paced the length of the bus stop with much more purpose than a boy of twelve should have. My thoughts did not move forward as much as trip over themselves like so many drummers in an ill-prepared marching band. These awkward thoughts were accompanied by another, more elegant one, woven like a secret gold strand into the loose twill of my mind. Even after I had boarded the bus, I could not stop thinking how grown up I was. I knew a gunshot victim. In fact, I was the only kid at school who knew what had happened. Every other time I had returned to I.S. 70 after a school holiday, I had dreaded the journey as much as I dreaded the day that lay at its terminus. This morning, I actually looked forward to attending O. Henry School; this time I had a tale to tell, something no other kid—no matter how cool, how rich, how popular—could match. At the same time, I felt horribly guilty about this pleasure.

On the bus I told each kid who boarded about the incident, using the weight of its seriousness to shield myself from the usual litany of snaps and jokes about my old sneakers. The truth was that I experienced a tiny burst of joy every time I got to tell someone what had happened, followed by a wave of panicky guilt, much as one savors the sweetness of a bite of ice cream, then reels from the headache that ensues. By then I considered Jerome my best friend, though I was probably not alone. He was one of the most popular kids at I.S. 70, even among the whites, just as he seemed to be loved by everyone back in the projects. But when his accident happened, his mother had chosen me and my family to receive the news first. I was the Source; I was the Word. It didn't matter that I was the only white boy among the commuters.

"Stop foolin'," I remember Matt imploring. His brown, freckled grin stayed put, as if by smiling long enough he could lighten up the situation by sheer force of will. Instead, his grin took on a clownish, macabre air as he slowly realized that I was in no way kidding.

"I ain't jokin'," I said, with more of a confident inner city accent than usual. It was incomprehensible that Jerome could have been shot; I don't think it had actually happened in any of our minds yet. To me Jerome was still the Defender champion, the skinny kid with the big smile who my sister adored. He wasn't a gunshot victim, lying close to death. That was just the hype, the talk. So it was no matter for me to score points off his accident when people asked. It was so abstract, all it meant for me that day was that for a few hours, I wasn't the honky anymore.

I told how it happened many times that day. "He was just walking down Avenue D," I would say. "And *boom*," I added for emphasis, before shifting tone and rhythm. "Actually"—I would cough and correct myself each time for effect—"there was no boom; there was no sound, no light, no nothing." I paused again. "Jerome fell face down onto the sidewalk. 'Quit foolin',' the person next to him said." The story got better each time I told it; later in the day it became " 'Quit foolin',' *we* said." No one at that school lived on Avenue D except Jerome, me, and a few others, so no one challenged my account. I described the exact location, detailing each boarded-up building and its potential for housing snipers. "They think it was a ricochet," I added to wind up my tale, crossing my arms in a gesture of self-satisfaction.

The truth was, I was nowhere in the vicinity when the bullet hit Jerome's neck. I was home, sleeping. My mother never

let us out of our apartment on major holidays. Her usual paranoia over safety reached its highest pitch on the Fourth of July,
Chinese New Year, and December 31. She would cook my sister and me whatever we wanted to eat, let us watch as much
television as we wanted, even allow us to drink soda on those
most dangerous nights of the year. Alexandra and I would guz-
zle down Mountain Dew, Diet Pepsi, or some other forbidden
nectar as my mother quoted emergency-room mortality statistics to us. We rolled our eyes, feeling like refugees with care
packages in our detention center of an apartment, watching
from behind barred windows while the explosions of celebra-
tion went on all around us. Not until the days *after* major cele-
brations were we allowed outside to play; those dates my
mother considered some of the safest of the year, since they
found everyone at home nursing hangovers. To Alexandra and
me, July 5 was Independence Day, and the New Year didn't
start until sunrise on January 1.

However, in 1982 the forces of violence proved too strong
for even my mother's logic. We got the phone call from
Jerome's mother, who asked if his sister Zuni could stay with
us for a while. My mother, who answered the call, started to
cry, which she rarely did. After returning the receiver to its
cradle, she kept thanking her nameless God that it hadn't been
either Alexandra or me. She ran over to hug us and cried for a
while longer; my sister joined in, even though she and I had yet
to learn what was wrong. I didn't say anything; my mind was
racing through all the people I loved, wondering who had
died. Finally she told us, and the roulette wheel in my mind

stopped spinning. I didn't think anything; my brain was totally numb in a way it never has been since.

Jerome couldn't have visitors right away, so critical was his condition. Not until a few days later, after that first day back at school, did I go to Saint Vincent's Hospital to see Jerome and learn the reality of the situation. My family wouldn't be able to visit Jerome until later, so I went alone. Saint Vincent's stood just a couple of blocks south of Fourteenth Street, so the ambulance must have taken almost the exact route that the bus traversed on our way to school. Since Jerome's situation had been an emergency, I went to the emergency room. All I found there was a lone pregnant woman, who moaned in cadence with the talk show that played overhead on an encaged television set. I lingered and gawked for a moment before continuing my search.

I finally found the front desk. The staff issued me a huge pass the same green color as the security guards' polyester blazers. The awkward, Alice-in-Wonderland dimensions of the pass served clearly to demarcate the visitors from those individuals with official roles, making me feel all the more childish at a time when I was gearing myself up to be as adult as possible. I got out of the elevator at the eighth floor, pediatrics. The walls were a faint yellow, decorated with exotic animals that would never have survived in North America, let alone in New York City. Zebras marked one door, cockatoos another, always in twos, as if this were Noah's Ark, saving all creatures great and small from the flood. Jerome's room, when I found it, was marked by a pair of green alligators.

I pushed the door open tentatively. Inside, Jerome's mother sat holding his hand and crying. She was rocking back and forth as if in the middle of a Jewish prayer, sitting up on a plastic-covered green chair that had been extended to form a bed. "My poor baby," she said, repeating over and over: "My baby's paralyzed." White sheets were twisted up into a rope-like strand on the chaise. Jerome's mother straddled the ottoman part of the seat as she patted his hand. Kids, most of whom I didn't recognize, stood around the two of them, not saying much, seemingly mesmerized by her rocking and the cadence of her voice. She didn't really weep but rather whinnied and whined as if she were having a bad dream.

The walls of the hospital room were covered by beige wallpaper that bore a repeating pattern of three clowns. One held a pinwheel, another waved a magic wand, and the third gripped a hoop through which a circus dog jumped. These pediatric touches seemed absurd, mocking even. The room was darkened, and in the dim light the clowns seemed almost to be laughing at the predicament in front of them. In their two-dimensional world, movement of limbs had never been an issue.

"My poor baby," Jerome's mother said over and over.

I was feeling a bit dizzy. I had slipped into the darkness of the room barely noticed, the way one might enter a Native American sweat lodge after the ritual had already begun. Soon after I arrived, two doctors strode into the room and asserted control over the situation by flipping on the light without warning, parting the group of kids around the bed, and taking Jerome's hand from his mother.

"I'm the surgeon," the first doctor introduced himself to Jerome, speaking loudly, the way people talk to foreigners. "How are you feeling?" he asked in a heavy Southern drawl. "Are you feeling okay?"

Jerome opened his eyelids—not in a heavy fashion, but alertly, as if he had been called on by the teacher to answer a question. "I'm fine," he said. This answer didn't halt the groans from his mother's lips; in fact, she got more upset the more in control Jerome appeared.

"I'm going to check your respiration and heart rate," said the other doctor in a tone that only lovers and medical practitioners use to announce what they are going to do before they do it. Her badge said that she was a pediatrician, and her careful manner seemed to have a calming effect on Jerome's mother. But just as she leaned over and was slipping the metal sensor under Jerome's hospital gown, a horrible voice came over the intercom. "Code 99," it said, so loudly that I couldn't imagine how any patient wouldn't jump out of bed. Jerome didn't even seem to hear it. "Pediatrics code 99," the voice said. "Room 824. Code 99. Code 99." The doctors rushed out of the room so rapidly it seemed as though the wallpaper clown had waved his magic wand and made them vanish. Outside the room, many white coats rushed past. Most were silent save the squeak of their sneakers on the linoleum tiles. Following the staff that had flown by came a technician dressed in green pushing a big machine as another white-clad doctor rubbed what looked like the lids of two pots together.

After this machine had passed, there followed a silence in both the hallway and our room that lasted until Jerome's mother started up again. "My poor baby," she said, much more quietly now. Maybe she didn't want to disturb the resuscitation efforts that were going on down the hall; or maybe they seemed to her an omen and jolted her anew into worry. "My poor baby's paralyzed."

Jerome, for his part, sat propped up about 45 degrees by the bed and a couple of pillows. He seemed strangely unperturbed by all that was going on around him. It was as if someone had stripped off all the features of his personality and gotten him down to the bare minimum. He seemed like his essence, his most basic self, but at the same time completely different, like a chair that is still recognizable as a chair even though it has lost all four of its legs and its back. In this stripped-down state he seemed calmer and wiser than all of us around him. For me the whole scene was all too chaotic, too confusing—in short, too much to handle. I felt as though I were caught in the ether of one of my nightmares, running but not running up the stairwell or afraid but calm as I hovered, treading air outside our twenty-first-floor window. No one spoke except Jerome's mother, her phrase rolling over and over, casting its hypnotic spell over the room: "My baby's paralyzed . . . "

I needed to feel the reality of the situation, to make sense of it. The only way my twelve-year-old mind knew how to do this was to focus on rational details, so I finally asked, "Is it from the neck down or the waist down?"

My voice cracked when I said this. I seemed to have snapped his mother's litany, for she turned to me and said, in the most dignified manner, "I do not think that is an appropriate question at this time." She said it with the intonation of a question, an upward lilt at its end that made me feel even worse for having asked. After her interjection the other visitors, mostly teenagers, hissed and *psss-chaw*ed at me, echoing her sentiments. Jerome, though still conscious, didn't say anything one way or another, and I slunk out of the room, my usual discomfort at being the only white person in the crowd magnified tenfold by the reaction to my comment. Or perhaps my discomfort over their response was magnified tenfold by the fact that I was white. Either way, the result was the same, and I got out of there quick.

The next time I visited Jerome in the hospital, I tried to make amends by not mentioning his condition. I only talked about how lame school was. Unable to bear going alone, I brought my mother and sister with me. They flitted around the room, arranging bouquets and making small talk. My mother taped his get-well cards and photos around the room at eye-level so he could see them. Meanwhile, my sister hovered over him like a hummingbird, dropping McDonald's french fries into his open mouth as if he were her baby nestling. I just sat in the corner of the room the whole time, picking at a blemish on my face until it bled, praying they wouldn't ask him the same thing I had.

At the end of the fall semester, a couple weeks before he took the bullet, Jerome had turned over the Defender video game machine at the Twin Donut on Fourteenth Street—that is, he had racked up more than 99,999 points, thereby causing the machine to reset itself to zero. He had told me about this feat, the highest achievement in video gaming, shortly before I heard the terrible news. I went to the Twin Donut, which I hadn't visited since my mother had dragged me out by the ear. On the machine I saw his initials carved in silicon, listed among the top ten scorers. I felt a pain in my stomach at the sight of his initials and vowed never to play Defender again.

Back in the projects, Jerome's absence and my inopportune question about the extent of his paralysis had ruined all the mending that had occurred between the community and me. I reverted to taking the back route in and out of my building. In fact, I regressed quite a bit in my sociability more generally, since I was becoming ashamed of my appearance. It was as if the gunshot that had wounded Jerome also signaled the start of puberty for me. My entire body felt out of sorts, as if different parts were growing at different speeds and I was left with the task of reconciling the whole. I sprouted hair from every possible pore and spent increasing amounts of time in the bathroom plucking, squeezing, and exfoliating. I now wore thick glasses and started to develop a case of acne, though not as severe as my father's had been. With each new pimple or patch of hair, I uncovered a whole new area of insecurity. Each time I looked in the mirror—and at ages eleven and twelve there were many such times—I saw my changing body as something distinct from what I called myself. As a result I didn't know what "myself" was anymore. Then my mind would skip like a record needle to Jerome; I'd wonder what it must feel like to go through puberty with a paralyzed shell of a body. Each time I thought of his motionless form, I felt that same trapdoor open up in my stomach as when Sean had followed me that day after school.

After visiting Jerome a couple more times in the hospital, I found I could no longer bear the pediatric ward, and being in his presence disturbed me. I felt nauseous and dizzy when we were making small talk. I was still a bit dazed over what had happened to him, and this feeling synergized with the new insecurities of adolescence to produce some very strange behavior. I developed a full-blown obsessive-compulsive disorder. I forbade everyone from kissing me at all; only I could kiss them, and I had to do it twice on each cheek, to protect them from tragedies such as had befallen Jerome. If I messed up the symmetry, I would say "Cancel, Cancel" and start over. If I were kissed, the spell would be broken and something violent might happen to my loved ones; as a result, after Jerome's accident no one kissed me for quite some time. My family members decided it would be easier to cooperate with my superstition than to try to reason me out of it.

"I'm in a hurry," my father would say on his way to the racetrack. "Give me the Daily Double, quick." I would turn his stubbly, scarred cheek to one side and give him two quick pecks. Then, with the control of a barber giving a shave, I would swivel his chin and kiss the other side twice. My compulsion didn't stop with the Daily Double, however; soon the kisses spread like brushfire to anything and everything in the house. Animate or inanimate, I kissed it all. I crawled around the stained green carpet on my hands and knees, kissing the furniture and plants before leaving for school. I had to get up earlier each day, since it now took twenty minutes to leave the apartment. At school and on the bus I didn't kiss anything, but I had to keep everything symmetrical. If I bumped the edge of my right foot on the leg of the desk, I had to bump the identical spot on my left foot, then the right again, then the left, so it totaled two times on each side. When I ate anything it had to be in fours—two bites on each side of my mouth. I spent my lunch hour eating my lima beans or corn very slowly, counting the number of remaining kernels or bits or kibbles when I got close to the bottom of the bowl, so I could be sure to say "Cancel, Cancel" before eating the last four. I spent much of my school day drowning in a bundle of tics and twitches not much different from those I had while attending the black class at the Mini School.

My mother sent me to a sliding-scale therapy clinic that cost us five dollars a week. I must have been trying to recover a sense of psychic control over my body while Jerome was going through real physical therapy. The sessions didn't help, however, largely because I hardly ever talked about Jerome or his accident. I felt it would have been belittling to Jerome to talk about him as an aspect of my clinical condition. After a while the therapy ended, and my mother turned to more traditional methods—nailing a mezuzah up on our door jamb.

She convinced me to try and focus all my non-human kisses on this religious icon, the first ever to grace our abode. Within a couple of weeks I managed to rein myself in and keep my Daily Doubles confined to the mezuzah and the people I loved, sparing the furniture.

This obsession remains with me to this day. I still kiss my loved ones twice on each side. I am never kissed back if I can help it. I still do lots of things, ranging from exercise to swallowing juice, in quiet sets of two or four. The need comes on more strongly at some times than at others. Compared to what befell Jerome, it is a small scar to carry through life. Nonetheless, it is a very real remnant of the violence that beset our neighborhood in the early 1980s.

One afternoon, my need to do everything in sets of two not only failed to protect me but actually put me in danger. I had restarted karate for the first time since Rahim's death; the class met after school on Mondays and Wednesdays. The *dojo* was located in the building where Raphael, one of my few remaining friends at I.S. 70, lived. Raphael, who attended karate with me, was a different type of Latino from those I had known previously, the first minority individual I had met who confounded the overlap of race and class. He was well off. His mother was a Colombian citizen, his father a white American with a ponytail. Though his parents were artists like my own, they had made the wise investment choices that my parents had forsaken. They lived in the up-and-coming Chelsea area, just north of school, in a loft probably not too different from the one my parents had considered in Soho years back. Raphael was one of the largest kids in school but, like Jerome, one of the most soft-spoken.

Karate class began at five o'clock, so Raphael and I spent the interim two hours running around the neighborhood, playing board games, or chatting up his building's elevator operator, who told us how he'd killed men with his bare hands during World War II. Raphael and I were the only nonadults in the class, and he was the only non-white member. There were no prayerful bowings to Mecca, no trips to tournaments situated in faraway mosques. So despite being the smallest person in the group, always matched up against a much larger opponent, I wasn't as nervous here as I had been in the other class.

My symmetry tics did get in the way sometimes, making my punches and kicks somewhat predictable. On the other hand, the patterning of my movements meshed well with the underlying philosophy of the tae kwon do and kendo styles we were learning, and the counting provided a rhythm to my *katae* and my freestyle fighting that had been lacking. The patterns became increasingly complex, moving from twos to fours to eights and sixteens and ultimately to thirty-twos, with each movement doubled, once for each side of my body. Also, this obsession with evenness made me a much better left-handed chopper and puncher than I otherwise would have been.

For the most part, the afternoons Raphael and I spent awaiting karate class were unsupervised, with his parents away at jobs or studios. They always had some delicious, rice-based Colombian leftovers in their restaurant-style silver refrigerator, along with a pitcher of Hawaiian Punch. In this after-school cuisine, Raphael seemed to reflect his bicultural heritage in a way that I had never managed to balance in my choices between my father's WASPy Hellmann's mayonnaise and my mother's Jewish Miracle Whip.

One day we decided to play "fireman, waterman," a game Raphael had invented. When he explained the rules to me, I instantly requested to be fireman. It was my job to whip matches off a pack, striking them in the same singular motion with which I hurled them like burning spears at Raphael. His job was to spray water on them and me with a mister that his mother kept around for the house plants. I won—and won big. I whipped matches off left and right, quite literally, looking like some strange kind of martial artist as I chased him in my karate outfit. A couple of times I stung the exposed portion of his forearm with the smoldering ember, scoring points as he retreated into his bedroom.

I pressed my attack onward as he climbed up into his loft bed, where he could maintain a better defensive position. I was aggressive with the matches, releasing frustration, gaining a sense of freedom I hadn't felt since Jerome's accident. Raphael was already hopping down from the loft bed when I threw a second match in that direction. I knew I would miss him with that shot, but that didn't matter: I had to do each attack in doubles. Several minutes later my ammo ran out, and we went to his parents' room at the other end of the loft to look for a fresh book of matches. It was Raphael's turn to play the role of fireman; he headed back toward the kitchen, while I filled up the water bottle in the sink near his mother's work space.

He ran back to me, screaming.

"Fire!" he yelled in a voice so loud that its volume obscured his slight accent. He didn't sound serious, but he didn't quite sound like he was kidding either.

"Fire!" he yelled again.

I laughed and squirted him with cold water.

"Fire!" he yelled, blinking from the mist. He ran back toward his bedroom, and I followed him very slowly, still playing the game and wary of being lured into a trap. Then I saw it. Black, black smoke curled up, running along the old tin ceiling as if it were caressing the fine craftsmanship. I walked a little farther and saw that the whole back side of his apartment was in flames.

"Fire!" he screamed again and again, I don't know how many times. I still said nothing and kept walking toward his room, from which it all seemed to originate. I had never seen such a big fire, not even at Boy Scout camp, where we constructed a huge, two-story bonfire to celebrate the end of the summer. This was different. It was not something controlled.

As I neared the bedroom, I could feel the warmth of the flame on the skin of my chest, which was exposed by the loose-fitting gi. The fire had spread in a seemingly random pattern, picking and choosing what it liked for tinder. Its selections were not always obvious ones. Against one wall rose a multicolored sheet of flame, blue-red-orange. It took me a second to make out the item underneath this gaseous rainbow: Raphael's backpack, readied for a father-son camping trip that weekend, each of its component materials glowing in a different part of the light spectrum. Next door, the kitchen countertop burned slowly, more ember than actual flame, looking like some new type of indoor barbecue grilling device. A white plastic stool had wilted in one corner, its four legs melted down as if it had fainted from exhaustion. The round seat flickered as it shriveled down to some essence of concentrated plastic, giving off much more inky smoke than would seem possible from such a small, withered item.

"Fire!" I heard Raphael yell. He must have been running past me, and quickly, since I made out the Doppler shift in his voice. That always reminded me of the sirens speeding by twenty-one flights below my bedroom window.

"Fire!" he screamed again, now in the hallway of his building. Before I was aware that any time had passed, the sweeping motion of a huge adult male arm scooped me up. It felt as though I were being yanked from the stage on the *Gong Show*. The arm belonged to our karate teacher, who swung me around with the same grace he used in class, planting me down in the stairwell, just outside the threshold of the loft, beyond the doorway that marked the entrance to the apartment.

"911!" he yelled as he rushed back inside with the fire extinguisher, dressed up in his white *gi* and black belt. The elevator operator gave him a perfunctory salute and rang emergency services from the phone in his prewar lift. Now that adults were on the scene and things were actually happening, Raphael stopped yelling, and we both stood peering into the loft, craning our necks to follow the *sensei*'s efforts while obeying his implicit instructions to stay out. He seemed to be having some trouble getting the fire extinguisher to work. Pathetically short streams were squirting out intermittently from the tip of the hose, landing just a few inches in front of the silver canister, accomplishing less than Raphael's spray bottle would have. After a moment or two he got it to flow properly, but it didn't make much difference. He was able to put out the backpack and the countertop but not much else. Whenever the stream hit a flaming object or section of the wall, plumes of white smoke rose from the area, mingling with and soon overpowering the black smoke that had preceded it. The white smoke gave off the balmy feeling of steam, along with a strange mélange of odors produced by the burning nylons and polyesters and plastic-like substances.

Not too much later the firemen arrived. They marched up the stairs with big loping steps, as if their black rubber boots had been made for fly-fishing and not firefighting. Their business-as-usual air verged on boredom, as if we had roused them from a nap at the station house for something that was more inconvenience than emergency. They hooked up their hoses to a water line in the hallway and then plodded into the apartment, the beige, canvas-covered firehose tracing the path along which I had pressed my assault on Raphael. One yelled to another to cut on the water, and then gallons upon gallons poured onto the flaming and smoldering objects. The entire apartment and hallway filled up with steam of the same stale flavor that emerges from manhole covers in the streets.

Soon we were all covered in beads of condensed water vapor, each drop the distilled essence of what used to be Raphael's family's belongings. I crawled up the stairs and huddled in the dark at the next landing, tucking my head between my knees and gripping them as tightly as I could, trying to pull myself into the smallest ball possible, to fold myself out of existence. In this position I rocked back and forth on the top step.

Somehow word of the fire reached our parents, and the next thing I noticed was my mother standing before me on the stairwell. She reached to me as I had to Marcus after pummeling him. I took her hand and she tugged me up. She yanked me straight into a hug, which shocked me so much that I flinched as she pulled me toward her. I pressed my cheek into her bosom, and she kissed my sooty hair, the first time I had been kissed since the beginning of my obsessive-compulsive disorder. Her reaction did not fit into the punishment paradigm; she merely appeared glad that I was safe and sound. Not an iota of anger or judgment entered her expression or tone of voice as she cooed to me that everything would be okay. Given the seriousness of what had happened, this lack of castigation overwhelmed me, and I started crying. I don't know how long I went on sobbing, but eventually she spoke.

"Tell them what happened," she instructed, nodding to a newly arrived set of fire officials, who wore clean, pressed uniforms and ties. They listened as I explained what we had done. Raphael was nowhere to be seen; evidently they had already questioned him separately. His father listened silently as the city officials enunciated every syllable of each question. After each thing I said, they jotted something down while simultaneously asking, "Then what happened?" A series of these questions led me through the entire afternoon, until I wound up at that very moment when we were standing there. I did not volunteer my certainty that I knew exactly which match had caused the fire—the one I threw after Raphael had jumped down from his bed; the one I threw to make things symmetrical.

The whole time I was telling the story, I kept thinking that I had financially ruined my parents; they, not me, would be held accountable. Thinking this made me feel worse but also, in my mind, justified my hedging about the truth. At the end of my tale, Raphael's father spoke. "Did Raphael light any matches?"

"Yes," I said, truthfully; Raphael had lit one match to demonstrate the arm motion to me. That match was certainly not the cause of the fire, since he never threw it, but I knew this would muddle the morality of the situation. I was right. Raphael's father went into the apartment and pulled Raphael out by his blackened *gi* sleeve.

"You both lit matches, you are both equally responsible for this mess," he said. They were magic words. Raphael must have felt the same sense of sole guilt that I did, since he didn't protest at all when his father issued this judgment. Perhaps he blamed himself for having suggested the game in the first place, or maybe he felt he'd failed as the waterman.

His father led us on a tour of the wreckage. The fire itself didn't seem to have done as much damage as the smoke and water had. He pointed to various things that were destroyed, frowning silently. But whenever he did speak, his statement was upbeat. "Thank God it didn't reach the other end of the loft, where your mother's paintings are," he said at the start of our walk-through, adding that, in one way, it was lucky the sprinkler system hadn't activated, since it would have ruined her work. A few paces later he added, "Thank God it didn't spread to the other floors."

He thanked God several more times until we reached Raphael's charred loft bed and his sleeping bag, which had been readied for their weekend camping trip but now sat shrunken into what looked like a charred, rolled-up newspaper. Pointing to this, he yelled, raising his voice above a New Age monotone for the first time: "What if one of you had been in there? What if one of you had been in there?"

He cried; then Raphael cried; I fidgeted and trembled, tapping the floor in counts of two.

The fire department seemed to follow the same logic as Raphael's father, deciding that if we both had lit matches then we were both to blame—and therefore no one was to blame. They declared the fire an accident, and I received no state-sanctioned reprimand; as a result of this ruling, the insurance company had to pay up. My parents seemed relieved that I hadn't been found officially culpable, that Raphael's parents were not going to press us for money we didn't have, that I wouldn't have to face proceedings that would have affected my life chances, that I wouldn't have legal scars that wouldn't be expunged from my file when I moved on to high school. Their relief seemed to stitch with mine into one collective web of familial guilt, preventing me from receiving punishment. In private I explained to them that I knew I had caused the actual fire, but they didn't seem to care, as if the person with the gun were no more to blame than the person who dared him to shoot.

"You've learned more than we can teach you from this," my father said while squinting to make out the fine print in his *Racing Form*. Then he looked up from his calculator and pile of pens. "More than we can teach you," he repeated. He went back to his calculations, and that was all he ever said about the incident.

For some time hence, I continued to be baffled by this logic, by the fact that my worst crime brought me the least punishment. This irony didn't escape my sister either; whenever she got into trouble after that, she invoked the memory of the fire. "I can't believe I'm in trouble for not cleaning my room! You're actually going to punish me when *Dalton*," she would say, uttering my name with a snide dip in tone, "*Dalton* can burn down apartment buildings for nothing. It's not fair! It's not fair!"

She was right. It wasn't fair—and the unfairness went far beyond matters of sibling rivalry. Even at the time of the event I knew that had the fire not been in Chelsea but down the street from our house in one of the row tenements that lined Avenue D—or had I been of a different skin tone—the whole matter might not have been settled so casually. In that case the fire itself would not have been lesson enough for me—at least, not according to the police and fire departments. The fire taught me one of the most subtle but powerful privileges of middle-class status: the chance to work problems out informally, without the interference of the authorities. Poor minorities get no such allowances. But we were lucky—for Raphael's family represented the right class and I the right race.

Not only does the government deprive low-income families of the opportunity to take care of their own kids and their own mistakes, it actively goes after them in the form of drug raids, weapons sweeps, and other such policy initiatives. I learned this a few years later, when one of my neighbors from Masaryk was busted in a drug raid. Because he had recently turned eighteen he was tried as an adult, and because of new mandatory minimum sentencing he was given twenty-five years of hard time, while the average murderer serves five years. Marc, the son of a Piratas coach, is still in prison to this day, his life ticking away slowly, another type of victim of the war on drugs. I remember Marc as the kid who used to pump me up with confidence, telling me that because I batted left-handed I had a chance to be like the greatest home-run sluggers of all time. I remember the freckle that sat like an exotic accent on his upper lip, just above his smile. And I remember how many unpaid hours his father volunteered to run the team. The next time Marc will be able to visit home or watch a Piratas game or just slurp an icie, he will be in his forties. I, by contrast, learned enough of a lesson from the fire itself.

As I had originally anticipated, my whole life soon started afresh. Not long before Jerome was shot, I had taken a high school admission test along with almost every other eighth grader in New York. Shortly after the blaze at Raphael's house, I was relieved to learn I had made it into one of the three academic schools and would not have to remain at I.S. 70 for another year. Thanks to standardized testing, my record of video-game truancy and pyromania meant nothing.

I had made it into the second most selective school, the Bronx High School of Science, which meant I faced a ninety-minute commute each morning and afternoon. To me, it was well worth taking three separate subway lines each way to escape facing Raphael and the rest of I.S. 70 each day for an additional year. My mother worried about such a long subway commute through heavily crime-ridden sections of the Bronx. She didn't like that I would have to get up before dawn and return well after dark during much of the autumn and winter. She quoted police statistics to me, claiming that the hours immediately preceding sunup were the most dangerous of all. I escaped this fate, however. Since I had missed the cutoff for the more competitive, Manhattan-based Stuyvesant High School by only a single point, and since I came from a low-income neighborhood, I qualified for a special summer school program that would allow me to make up the exam deficit and attend my first-choice school. This despite the fact that I hadn't actually attended school in our low-income neighborhood for seven or so years by virtue of our fake address.

School wasn't the only thing that was changing about my life. We were moving, too. When our karate teacher, Rahim, had been shot a few years earlier, my mother—unbeknownst to the rest of the family—had put us on the waiting list for a low-rent building on the west side of town. When Jerome was shot, she redoubled her efforts to get the family out of the neighborhood, which had just entered an epidemic of crack- and heroin-related gun violence. Gunshots had by then replaced fire-engine sirens as the aural trademark of urban blight. Historically speaking, the two sounds were not entirely unrelated. Many of the burned-out buildings that had resulted from landlord-arsonist collaboration during the 1970s now served as heroin-shooting galleries or crack houses for the new wave of urban ill.

Each charred tenement went through a cycle of ecological and economic development. First, weeds sprouted amid the wreckage. Then we younger kids explored and played in the unsafe, condemned structures. Then squatters replaced us— occasionally the same people who had been tenants of the building before it had burned down. In the final wave of succession, some of these former residences turned into crack houses in which people as burnt-out as the buildings themselves puffed on glass pipes full of the new drug. The rise of the crack trade in the early 1980s had spawned a new wave of neighborhood violence over profits. In fact, Jerome had been shot from the charred hole that passed for a window on the top floor of one of these former tenements.

"The old junkies never hurt anyone," my mother said, pining for the days when heroin had dominated the local scene. Giddily, she described how they fell asleep standing up, slowly ratcheting to one side until they almost fell over. "They nodded off on the bus, just like Weebles," the popular 1970s toy. "Then, just when you'd think they'd topple, *snap*, they would jerk themselves up. It was actually exciting watching them, wondering if they would fall over. It's different now; it's not the same with crack . . . "

Her voice trailed off. She was leading my sister and me on a tour of low-income housing on Roosevelt Island, a small atoll in the East River halfway between Queens and Manhattan. The apartments had been reserved for low-income residents as part of a tax deal cut by the development group, and Ellen had put our name on that waiting list as well, determined to get us out of the Lower East Side. My father, however, had no interest in leaving Manhattan.

"I'm not going to live on a prison," he had announced that morning without looking up from his *Racing Form* or breaking the rhythm of his constantly jiggling leg, which shook to the reggae wailing from his prized boom box. "I'm not going to be trapped in a white ghetto." His hand gripped his pen tighter and jerked it even more furiously as he squiggled red lines over last-minute scratches from the race lineups, horses with names like Onyxly or Sojourner's Truth. He went off to bet on maiden special weights, turf allowances, and $5,000 claimers, while Alexandra and I marched off to Roosevelt Island with our mother.

After Jerome was shot, my parents experienced acutely opposite reactions. While my mother's obsession with safety and her misgivings about our neighborhood reached a feverish pitch, my father grew increasingly attached to the area. He had learned how to project his fifty-yard stare like a lance, rivaling that of any of the men who strutted down Rivington Street. In fact, the boys who had started to come calling for my prepubescent sister called him Charles Bronson and claimed they would have visited more often if they hadn't been so scared of him. My father liked the pit bulls with spiked collars that cropped up like mushrooms around the neighborhood, dogs that displayed an ocular intensity to match that of their owners. He reveled in the Caribbean music that flooded the streets with the coming of the sticky summer weather. And he loved telling Puerto Rican jokes to Puerto Ricans. When one of my sister's new friends came over, Steve asked him straightaway, "Why can't Puerto Ricans barbecue?" When the thirteen-year-old chuckled nervously, claiming that he didn't know, my father responded: "Because the beans keep falling through the grill." The boy's mouth dropped, but when he saw my father's face turn red with laughter, he could not help but bust out giggling himself. The next time he visited, the two swapped jokes about Jews, WASPs, and the Irish, while my mother yelled in the background and my sister sat bored, twirling her hair into curls around a newly painted fingernail. I just looked on with envy, jealous of the kid, who interacted easily with my father, and of my father, who conversed with the kid in a relaxed way I never had.

"Words are meaning; words are truth!" my mother yelled in an out-of-breath voice. "Words hurt as much as sticks and stones."

"What's an Irish ten?" my father asked the kid, not even pausing for effect, but instead answering his own question with a giddiness he could not control: "A four with a six-pack."

The boy now gave my father a high five that wasn't so high as to hide it from my mother's view. "Word, nigger," said the kid, bestowing the title I had longed for onto my New England father.

"I heard that," my mother yelled from the other room. "You should never use the n-word. I don't care if everyone does. It's not right."

"Nigger, nigger, nigger!" my father yelled, giggling, his Charles Bronsonesque mug breaking up into a pudgy, child-like grin.

Jerome or no Jerome, Steve was having a good time and had no intention of leaving the neighborhood. Alexandra and I were on his side. We dragged our feet through the grass of Roosevelt Island after we had disembarked from the tram that served, at the time, as the only link between that small hunk of rock and the larger one called Manhattan.

My mother cooed at every sight. "Look," she said, pointing to something I couldn't make out with my two-year-old eyeglasses. "A red-breasted robin!" She made it a point to remark on every animal that crossed our paths during the tour, from squirrels to chipmunks to blue jays. But there were no dogs allowed, just as there were no cars. My father had been right without even having seen the place. It felt like some sort of institution, a distant cousin to the Riker's Island correctional facility up the river. But unlike Riker's, Roosevelt Island gave off a repressed, formal aura more like the United Nations, which lay just across the river.

Luckily, we never had to face the prospect of arguing over Roosevelt Island; our names came up for an apartment in the West Village, at the very same address we had used to finesse my entrance into grade school. When we went to visit Westbeth that spring, it seemed to me the reverse image of our own building. Almost everyone was white, with a few black families who played the role of minority that we had back in our neighborhood. The apartment itself was a gigantic duplex. Standing on its parquet floors, staring out the huge barless windows or up at the twelve-foot-high ceilings, my sister and I felt small, as if we had regressed in our growth curves. I couldn't understand why we should get all this and not the maintenance men who were on their hands and knees during our visit, replacing a section of floor that had warped from humidity and age. Why us and not them, I couldn't stop asking myself. I wondered where they lived.

The answer, I learned, lay in the word *artist*. Westbeth, funded by the U.S. Department of Housing and Urban Development in conjunction with the National Endowment for the Arts, provided subsidized housing for artists of all kinds. My parents had made it past the internal review panel that evaluated all applications when they came to the top of the waiting list. First we had to be recommended by a current resident— the man whose address we had used to get me into P.S. 41. Then my parents had to provide letters of reference from eminent people in their respective fields, certifying that they were indeed artists in whatever sense that word carried.

It all seemed so absurd. I had never taken art very seriously, even though I had consumed a lot of it over the course of my childhood. As soon as I was old enough my parents took me to the galleries in Soho, keeping me on a harness and long leash so they could yank me back whenever I rushed up to some colorful work, my fingernails extended like talons. During the early 1970s conceptual art was coming into vogue, and several pieces both baffled and inspired me. Once I saw an entire show that consisted of pieces of ripped-up grocery cartons, each one for sale at $500. On the long walk back to our apartment I collected old pizza boxes and other sorts of cardboard, which I used to set up a gallery at home. I tore them into what I considered to be interesting shapes and then taped these signed works onto the walls of the bedroom my sister and I shared.

Then I invited my parents inside to browse and purchase these items, which averaged around a nickel apiece.

Another time, after I had outgrown the leash, our parents took Alexandra and me to a Vito Acconci opening. Acconci was a performance artist who, during this particular show, had himself installed under the floorboards of the gallery, where he muttered "Fuck you" over and over. Alexandra and I thought it was a looped tape, since his voice sounded exactly the same each time. But he was there in person, supposedly masturbating while he repeated this mantra. For our part, we were thrilled to hear those dirtiest of all curse words given the adult legitimacy we projected onto the art world. "Fuck you, fuck you, fuck you," we said in robot-like voices to each other and my parents. When my mother said we were not to speak that way, we yelled back in unison, like a couple of striking workers, "It's art; it's art; we're allowed, 'cause it's art!" My father then joined in, repeating the words himself and laughing as my mother begged him not to encourage us.

As an alternative, Ellen encouraged me to do my own performance piece whenever we went gallery hopping. I had recently learned from a friend how technicians induced telephones to ring themselves when they wanted to test whether they were working properly. So instead of running around the galleries yelling "Fuck you," I was sent off in search of the pay phones. I would make them ring and then slip off, trying to repress my giggling. Then my parents and I would watch as some black-clad patron or gallery official would answer the phone, making funny faces when they only got a series of beeps and then dead air. Even my mother snickered when people would yell in all sorts of European accents, "Hullo? Hullo? Are you there? Can you hear me?"

From this early indoctrination through many a "dumb-painter" joke told by my father, I learned that art wasn't something serious and lofty nor was it a scam, but rather something in between. So it was difficult for me to understand why artists had become an identifiable group, like the poor, who really deserved help.

We finally moved in that summer, before I started high school, just as the dynamics of delinquency and teenage pregnancy were about to start affecting my age cohort back on Avenue D. My father was the most resistant to the change of scenery, agreeing to move only if we sublet the other apartment under the table, just in case we wanted to move back at some point in the future. When he walked through the prospective new neighborhood, he sneered at the boutique shops and the foofy little dogs.

While everything was still in boxes, my mother forced me to knock on the door of the apartment across the hall "to make friends" with the teenage boy who lived there. To my great relief he wasn't home, but I left my name and apartment number with his mother, thinking that was the end of the matter. My mother wasn't satisfied. The next day I was pasting my scribbled charts and diagrams up on the new wall over my desk when my mother entered the room. "There's a bunch of kids hanging out downstairs in the courtyard," she announced, in the same tone she always used when she wanted me go down and join in the Spalding baseball games of the ex-Piratas. "Why don't you—"

"Because I don't want to," I interrupted her. I had heard their laughter and the music coming from their boom box. It was techno-sounding white music that I didn't recognize. But when my mother left the room, I peered out the window and recognized one of the guys in the group from I.S. 70.

After pacing my new room for a few more minutes, I went downstairs. Kahlil, the kid I knew from school, was probably Middle Eastern, with a brown tint to his skin that let him belong to the white group while still being a minority of sorts. He was positioned at the center of this circle of teenagers. They were all smoking cigarettes. In the projects almost no one smoked cigarettes; it just wasn't part of the youth culture. The only things lit up were Phillies blunts full of marijuana. Back there, malt liquor served the same social function that cigarettes did here. I sidled up to the dozen or so smoking kids and sat down on a concrete structure at the periphery of the clique, not quite sure what to do with my hands since I had no cigarette. I'm not sure whether anyone noticed I was there. A tall, blond kid who looked like a young David Bowie was talking. He wore a white t-shirt with a green checkered button-down shirt hanging loosely over it. He had rolled up its short sleeves in perfect 1950s fashion, to go with his blow-dried pompadour-styled coif.

"My mother says I'm supposed to call up this new guy who moved in across the hall," the Bowie lookalike said a few moments after I had arrived on the scene. My heart dropped; I couldn't say anything, let alone identify myself as the individual in question. The timing of his statement had been too perfect to be a coincidence; I froze, wondering whether he actually knew I was there.

"Who is he?" someone else asked.

He reached into his shirt pocket and pulled out the scrap of paper I had left with his mother the previous day. "Danton Connolly," he read slowly, mispronouncing my name at every syllable.

"Dalton Conley?" Kahlil asked. I felt my moment of entry into the conversation approaching. It was going to be easier than I had thought to introduce myself to the group.

"Yeah, could be, I guess," the other kid said and slipped the scrap back into his breast pocket. "Know 'im? Is he cool?"

He—and I—awaited a response. Kahlil thought for a moment. "He's socially awkward," he announced.

I didn't know what to do. In the split second it took to react, my mind formulated two choices. The first was to put on ghetto-speak and confront Kahlil. "What the fuck you saying, nigga?" I might interject as I popped up, chest barreled outward, my face twisted up in disgust, ready to throw down. After all, I felt more confident of my chances in a physical confrontation here than I ever had back on the Lower East Side. All the same, Kahlil was quite a bit bigger than me, so I moved on to the other choice, which came to me through the voice of my father. His WASP wisdom would urge me to laugh loudly and chime in: "Yes, indeed, I am quite socially awkward," thereby throwing the comment back onto Kahlil.

But I did neither. I slunk off my perch and shuffled quickly upstairs, as I had several times from the splintered benches back in the projects, hoping that Kahlil couldn't recognize my silhouette from behind.

It was the authoritative ring of his diagnosis—its serious, almost sympathetic tone—that cut into me. Upstairs I paced in circles like a dosed-up laboratory animal, wishing I were back in our old neighborhood, where at least I had my skin color to blame for not fitting in. After this encounter I settled into the same old reclusive routine I had followed back on Avenue D. I began to think that moving to the new neighborhood would do little for my social life, that my problem had not been my skin at all but what it contained. It all added up, as far as I was concerned. My sister and father had no problem relating to, and even dissing on, people of all creeds and colors. My mother floated blissfully through life, unaware of how eccentric she was with her mismatched socks and inside-out sweatshirts. She could strike up a conversation with anyone who crossed her path. I decided the problem was not race, class, or any other categorical factor; the problem was me. So I decided to take action. In order to aid my social life, I ordered a series of five subliminal cassettes produced by a hypnotist. I didn't care about the *Quit Smoking Now*, *Stop Procrastinating*, or *Lose the Weight* tapes; I only wanted the last two: *Cultivating a Winner's Attitude* and, even more intriguing, *How to Be Popular*. When they arrived I used my father's boom box to dub them onto blank cassettes and photocopied the accompanying documentation. Then I returned the entire package within the ten-day free trial period, writing "cancel" across the invoice and never paying a cent of the $79.95.

As I lay in my bed with headphones on, the crashing waves and sea gulls of the New Age music calmed me while the subliminal message of *How to Be Popular* seeped into my brain. In the documentation, the hypnotist claimed the tapes normally started to show effects after six weeks of daily use. When nothing changed in my life by the two-month mark, I didn't give up, but I began to worry that the hypnotic messages might have been equipped with a special safeguard—an encoded message telling those who had bootlegged the tapes that they would always be losers and amount to nothing.

It seemed that nothing and no one could rescue me from my social predicament, not even Jerome. He came to visit our family the fall after I had started Stuyvesant, motoring around in an electric wheelchair that he directed with one of his hands. White plastic braces covered both his wrists, so I finally knew the extent of his paralysis. It seemed as though he had regained slight use of his hands but not much else. Jerome made an extra effort to be nice to me, as if he remembered my inappropriate question that day in the hospital room and wanted to show that it was no big deal. But I still couldn't look him in the eye. I was too busy tracing the paths of my shoelaces as they wove through the holes in my new basketball sneakers.

I started to tell Jerome about how I was playing basketball in an after-school league now, then caught myself with the realization that he would never play ball of any kind. "You guys any good?" he asked, gracefully rolling over the lump in the conversation. "Won't be long before I'm dunking," he added and smiled broadly. I hadn't seen this smile since the last day we hung out together before he was shot. I was overcome with the memory and couldn't meet his gaze. I started to cry silently, gulping as if I were drinking something bitter. Jerome kept talking as if nothing were happening.

"Zuni's starting junior high now," he said. "She says hello. So does my mother."

"Tell her I miss watching the shows with her," Alexandra interjected, before launching into the theme song for *Good Times*, one of the sitcoms Zuni and my sister loved: *"Keeping your head above water, making a wave when you can . . ."*

Speaking over Alexandra's crooning, my mother asked how his recovery was going. He admitted it was going slowly. "But now I use the wheelchair access on the M14 bus," he added. "At first I was too embarrassed, but now I don't care."

"Great," my mother seemed like she was going to say something more, but Jerome continued.

"Yeah, now I can get around anywhere, pretty much." Jerome's voice took on an excited air. "I'm thinking of moving to California," he said. While he spoke, he tilted his head to the other side as if his huge smile weighed heavily on his neck, and he needed to shift the burden.

"Temporary layoff!" my sister was still singing. She hopped onto the arm of his wheelchair like an overly enthusiastic lounge singer, balancing herself with one arm and gripping the back of his chair for support. *"Good times! Easy credit rip-off!"*

My mother and I cringed. "Alexandra!" my mother said.

"It's alright," Jerome smiled, raising his hand slowly to pat my sister's leg as best he could.

"I want to be an actor," Jerome continued, smiling at my sister. "So why not live in L.A.?"

I thought he was kidding about moving and smiled through my tears at my shoes; it was more of a grimace than a grin. My sister stopped her warbling. "You in California?" she hooted while I re-counted the eyelets on my sneakers. "You going to be surfing, getting tan! Can I come?" Jerome laughed, along with everyone in the family—everyone except me. I couldn't understand how my sister could talk about hitting the waves and sunbathing with a quadriplegic black man, while my comment in the hospital a few years earlier had offended everyone. The rest of my family seemed to slide as smoothly across the racial and disability divide as Jerome did across our parquet floor in his motorized wheelchair. Smoothly, that is, until he reached the gray cement stairwell that led to the second floor of our duplex.

"You got another floor up there?" he asked, tilting his heavy head upward.

I nodded.

"Def," he said, using the word for "great" that was popular at the time. "I looked for you guys back at Masaryk," he added. "How come you all moved here?"

My mother spoke before anyone else could get a word in.

"We moved here because of you."

For the first time ever my entire family was silent.

I spent my high school years shuttling in and out of our new building, trying to remain undetected after that first encounter with the clique in the courtyard. Moving into a white enclave had done little to integrate me into local life. The new location did pay off for me, however, by facilitating my school-based social life. At Stuyvesant I became friends not with the wealthy Greenwich Village kids but with those from the working-class outer boroughs my parents had forsaken fifteen years earlier. These kids commuted hours longer than I ever did to get an education. Since I was now living in a nice neighborhood not too far from school, my house became a popular after-school destination. At Stuyvesant nerdiness seemed to level most racial boundaries, and the friends I had crossed ethnic and national boundaries.

Though I enjoyed high school much more than I.S. 70, by the end of it I, like Jerome, wanted to leave my family, Westbeth, New York City, and the entire East Coast. After graduating I left for the San Francisco Bay Area, where I attended the University of California at Berkeley. After I filled out the dorm application requesting a "party animal" for a roommate, my mother laughed and gave me a t-shirt depicting Spuds MacKenzie—the party dog from a Budweiser ad campaign—as a going-away present. I streaked some of my dark hair blond. I even bought a pink surfing t-shirt in order to fit in. Berkeley would be the next in a series of new starts, cultural reinventions of myself.

I arrived at the dorms—subliminal tapes in hand—after twelve hours of flight and two airplane changes. My ears crackled, recovering from rises and falls in cabin pressure, as I wandered around the residential complex with bags hanging off my torso and limbs. The dorms seemed a lot like the projects—they had the same youthful energy and devilishness about them—except everyone was white. From the buildings that surrounded the central quad, speakers propped up in windows blasted music of bands I barely recognized. Back on Avenue D, I had generally heard pieces of song drift up the twenty-one stories and into my room, mingling with police sirens and honking horns as I scribbled away at my desk or paced between the bookcase and the bunk beds. Now I was in the middle of it, and guitar solos showered me from all sides as I hauled my luggage to my assigned building.

As I walked the streets of Berkeley on my first day, I noticed that this university town was run down in a different way than New York. There were no buildings covered in graffiti or bags of garbage spilling out onto the street, just political posters peeling off the walls and lots of small-time consumer litter lining Telegraph Avenue, the main drag that led up to campus.

Hundreds of napkins and straws and scraps of food dotted the sidewalk. It seemed as though everyone thought that dropping one little cigarette butt or cellophane wrapper didn't matter, but it added up, making Telegraph dirtier than the Lower East Side. I thought back to the day when I brought Michael home for the first time, when disgust for my neighbors had risen in my throat in tandem with the hawk's descent. Only now did I realize that they were no different from these middle-class Californians.

I had never seen so much whiteness in one place. I had never seen so much blondness anywhere. I whipped my head back and forth to catch sight of passing girls, their hair pulled back into ponytails by clips or bows or elastic bands covered in crinkled velvet. They wore pastel shorts and very white t-shirts. Some of the shirts had Greek letters on them. The girls' legs were all lightly browned, as if by a rotisserie, and seasoned with little blond hairs. On their feet they wore what looked like shower sandals over white tube socks. When they walked each step seemed strained; their hips stayed level as they plodded across the smooth concrete, thigh muscles flexing visibly with each step. No one—male or female—swooped and dipped as they strolled; no side-to-side movement. Here people walked; they didn't strut.

At the same time Telegraph Avenue was decaying, it was also springing to life. Most of the storefronts were made of weather-worn wood, but every fourth one was a revitalized establishment with a steel-and-plastic facade and a backlit fluorescent sign for a national chain such as Mrs. Fields Cookies or

Miller's Outpost. The people flooding the streets were like the stores themselves. Some were aging hippies or young wannabes, while others kept their shirts neatly tucked into ironed shorts. Tourists with cameras dangling off their wrists perused the selection of t-shirts that proclaimed "Welcome to Berzerkeley" or that depicted the chemical structure of LSD. Colors seemed newer out here; even the air appeared clean, crisp, and thin, as if I were watching television on a Sony Super Trinitron. By contrast, the sooty humidity of New York had always reminded me I was in reality.

I couldn't sleep that first night, so shortly before midnight I hopped a clean, futuristic subway train down to MacArthur Boulevard in Oakland, which my roommate had said was a rough area. As I walked the poorly lit streets, I could feel my mother watching me over the Rockies, keeping tabs on my unsafe behavior. The Oakland neighborhood was lined with single-family homes. Each yard had a chicken-wire fence separating it from the next. I half expected to see a goat or a rooster pop out from around the back of one of the houses. The homes looked as if they had once been painted in bright reds, blues, and yellows but had since faded from years of intense sun exposure. These were the first nonbright colors I had seen in the short time since I had arrived in the state of California.

Out here the difference between rich and poor seemed to be temporal more than spatial. The poor of today seemed to live in the middle-class digs of yesteryear. There were hardly any graffiti to speak of and no burned-out buildings, only the occasional boarded-up house. The sparse tags that lined my path were scribbled in regular penmanship, not the contorted script of New York. And no one was hanging out in the streets, sipping Colt 45 through a straw. I would have to learn a whole new type of poverty out here, just as I would have to learn all over again what being middle class meant.

Many of the Berkeley students moved out of the crowded dorms and into these weather-worn Oakland houses after their first year, mimicking on a smaller scale the process of "gentrification" that was occurring all across urban America. Back in New York, white people were pressing eastward during the 1980s and 1990s in some sort of backward Manifest Destiny, pushing their way almost to the projects but not quite reaching Avenue D. In the face of such gentrification, real estate values rose, an advantage not for the people who lived there but rather for the developers who pushed them out, compressing the border between white and minority. By the end of the 1990s, the Mini School—long since shut down—had been converted into luxury apartment units.

However, the projects create a natural bulwark against the spread of real estate development any further eastward. Upper-middle-class white people may be able to crowd out the corner bodegas and Puerto Rican social clubs, but they cannot budge the mammoth buildings that make up Masaryk or the Samuel Gompers houses. So there will come a time when rich and poor will face off against each other, the poor with their backs against the East River, Avenue D having become the border, the no-man's land of sorts. Manhattan already has the most unequal income distribution of any county in the continental United States. It is also the most densely populated locality. It only seems inevitable that it will be here—if anywhere—that rich and poor will live next door to each other. Neighborhood may come to mean less as an indicator of class status, but at the same time, poverty may become harsher by virtue of the fact that the poor will be confronted by those who are well off—in their faces, in their neighborhood—on a daily basis.

A walk down my old street shows other changes as well. More Asian immigrants are moving in. The local bakery has been replaced by a communications store that sells beepers and cell phones and provides money transfer services to Latin America. New York poverty has gone international, as many people support families back in the Caribbean or Central America. Some things are still essentially the same, however. There is still a settlement house right next to my building. The old supermarket my mother loved to complain about is still there, now called Key Food. The luncheonette where I stole the Reggie Bars continues to exist, but the Holocaust-surviving proprietors are long gone. Most of all, there are still no jobs there. Production had already left the inner city when I was coming of age; now it is a distant memory, and there is no hope for its return. The neighborhood and its institutions may still act as stepping stones for some new immigrants, just as they did for my mother's ancestors a century before. However, for residents who have lived there for generations, stones may have a different connotation—namely the red, brown, and yellow bricks that serve to keep them back, away from the American dream, to ghettoize and warehouse people of color who don't fit into the new America.

Jerome escaped those buildings, moving to California as he said he would. He went to Los Angeles to make it as an actor and landed the lead role in a PBS movie whose main character was a quadriplegic. He now lives in Oregon. Michael also now lives on the West Coast, in San Francisco, playing keyboards for a rock band. I don't know what became of Marcus or Raphael. Ozan, I last heard, had gone to business school after graduating from Harvard. *Sesame Street* Sean now works as a night supervisor for a livery car company. Marc is still locked up with many years to go.

My sister experienced some wild teenage days of mild drugs and truancy, flunking out of high school for a time. But she was surrounded by enough protective influences that her teenage rebellion never gathered enough momentum to ruin her life chances, as it had for Marc. Alexandra eventually finished high school, then college. During most of those years she dated José Torres, Jr., son of the first boxing champion in Puerto Rican history, and got to experience the lifestyle of the Puerto Rican elite, including dinners with the island's governor, its U.S. congressmen, and various movie stars. After they broke up, Alexandra pursued a master's degree in arts administration. She now runs Soho Rep, a small theater company in New York City.

I myself now live a couple miles from where I grew up, in the Chelsea neighborhood of Manhattan, not too far from

Raphael's family's loft. I live there, in a booming real estate market, because as a white, middle-class man, I have the choice to live wherever I want in America—in any sort of ethnic enclave or in the whitest suburbs I can afford. I choose to live in New York despite the fact that I work in Connecticut, at Yale University. Traveling to an elite university a couple of hours away reminds me of my daily jaunts across town to P.S. 41—except that now I have learned not to be as intimidated as I was that first day in third grade.

I cannot help but see my two-hour commute as a metaphor for the dynamics of race and class in America. When I speed up the Merritt Parkway and feel a surge of acceleration in my gut, I experience an unparalleled rush of freedom. I can go anywhere as long as I have some gas left in the tank. But if one were to pull back and take an aerial view of the ebbs and flows of traffic, the image would change dramatically. From a helicopter, traffic flows seem absurdly constrained and rhythmically patterned. Masses of cars lunge and recoil according to some not-so-complicated algorithm. Pulling back even further, we would notice that roads cover only a small portion of the earth's surface. From above, we don't appear to have much choice in where we are going, or how fast we can get there, but that does not deny each driver's experience of freedom and agency. It's the same with race and class. When I look back on my life and that of my neighbors, I cannot say that it was racism that got Jerome shot or that landed me in Stuyvesant or that sent Marc to prison. Nor can I conclude definitively that it was class that propelled me to the school district across town or got me off the hook when I burned down Raphael's apartment. Maybe I happened to change lanes just in the nick of time to avoid an accident; perhaps a traffic cop happened not to see me when I pulled an illegal maneuver. But when I add up all these particular experiences—as I have done in this book—the invisible contours of inequality start to take form, like the clogged traffic arteries of I-95.

My life, like anyone's, is only a sample of one, hardly statistically generalizable. But on my nonteaching days at Yale I run mathematical models on my computer in pursuit of that statistical certainty—trying to understand in some scientific way the leitmotif of race and class that has dominated my life. I have based the majority of my work on one particular interview study. It is a survey given to more or less the same set of 5,000 families each year for the last three decades. In fact, this data set and I are almost exactly the same age. So when I develop a computer model to predict what conditions in 1969 led to educational success or economic security in the 1990s, I am perhaps driven by the comforting feeling that the answers to my own life and those of my neighbors are just one keystroke away. But of course, they never are. What's gained in story is lost in numbers.

I want to take a moment to comment on the genre of memoir as applied to this particular volume. I believe this is an especially important task given my day job as social scientist. While *Honky* is a work of nonfiction—a sociological one at that—to some extent I am constructing a reality, as all memoirists are. In re-creating the characters, scenes, and dialogue of *Honky,* I am a captive of my own selective memories and those of my family members and my former neighbors. As a consequence, *Honky* does not meet the standards of evidence to which ethnographies are held; however, it has its compensating virtues. The greatest of these is the depth of understanding attained when one is more participant than observer—that is, when one spends many consequential—even formative—years of one's life in a social setting, rather than swooping in from afar to gather data for a time before going home to dinner and one's real life. Since *Honky* is based on lived experience, it is as much about what is not understood as it is about what is grasped. It is about the sense-making of children more than professionals. In short, it is about literary truths, not scientific ones.

A project like this would not have been possible without the help of many institutions and individuals. I would like to express my gratitude to some of them. Starting with the big and impersonal, I was fed, housed, and clothed by two academic institutions while writing this book; they are the University of California at Berkeley (specifically, the Robert Wood Johnson Scholars in Health Policy Research Program) and Yale University (in particular, the Institution for Social and Policy Studies and the Department of Sociology). While these institutions were primarily funding me to do other work, I hope they are satisfied that—in some small way—*Honky* contributes to their mission, broadly conceived.

Many people—both formal and informal reviewers—read drafts and provided helpful comments along the way; I am grateful for these efforts, and the book is better for it. They include Tara Bahrampour; Nina Chaudry; Mitchell Duneier; Sharon Hays; my spouse, Natalie Jeremijenko; Eric Klinenberg; my agent, Sydelle Kramer; Jonah Raskin; José Saldivar; Jacqueline Stevens; and Mayer Vishner. At the University of California Press, I am indebted to my editor, Naomi Schneider, for supporting yet another of my projects and for her vision, which helped lead the project from proposal to manuscript. I am also thankful to Larry Borowsky, the copy editor, who challenged many of my assumptions, both literary and sociological. I am particularly indebted to the production editor, Jan Spauschus Johnson, who not only managed the project from start to finish, but who also served as co–copy editor, brainstormer, and all-around facilitator. Her contribution was both technical and intellectual.

For the personal support I have received I am grateful to my family of origin, who put up with endless questions ranging from needling interviews to fact checks. Though you already know their names from the text, I repeat them here: Alexandra Conley, my sister; Ellen Alexander Conley, my mother; Stephen Conley, my father; and Sylvia Alexander, my grandmother. I am also grateful to some individuals—particularly mothers—from my old neighborhood, who patiently endured my repeated queries. Finally, I want to thank my family of destination, which, besides Natalie, is composed of E, my daughter, and Yo, my son.

Text:	12/16 Perpetua
Display:	Arial, Frutiger, and Industria
Design:	Steve Renick
Composition:	Binghamton Valley Composition
Printing and binding:	The Maple-Vail Book Manufacturing Group